Redefining Psychic Intelligence

Unleash Your PsyQ

Your Introduction to the
PsyQ Consultant
Home Experience

with

Martyn Pentecost

mPowr Publishing

©2019 mPowr Publishing

First Published in Great Britain 2019 by mPowr (Publishing) Limited

www.mpowrpublishing.com
www.whatsmypsyq.com

A catalogue record for this book is available from the British Library
ISBN – 978-1-907282-18-8

Design and Illustrations by Martyn Pentecost
mPowr Publishing 'Clumpy™' Logo by e-nimation.com
Clumpy™ and the Clumpy™ Logo are trademarks of mPowr Limited

Made by Book Brownies!

Books published by mPowr Publishing are made by Book Brownies. A Book Brownie is about so high, with little green boots, a potato-like face and big brown eyes. These helpful little creatures tenderly create every book with kindness, care and a little bit of magic! Before shipping, a Book Brownie will jump into the pages—usually at the most gripping chapter or a part that pays particular attention to food—and stay with that book, always. This means that every mPowr Publishing book comes with added enchantment (and occasional chocolate smudges!) so that you get a warm, fuzzy feeling of love with the turn of every page!

ONE THERAPY

CONTENTS

www.
whats
my
psya
.com

INTRODUCTION

The realms of psychic mediumship, mind control and superhuman abilities are steeped in mystery. So intricately woven with dogmatic religious beliefs are these, we see these abilities as something to fear or runaway from.

Blinded by thoughts of ghosts, demons and even worse, the darkest recesses of humankind, some avoid their innate power, whilst others dismiss any form of ability in this area as pseudoscience, fakery or charlatanism. Those who do embrace their *special gifts* are often such an elite (not through their abilities, but though the misconception of what these abilities are), they are given immense control over others.

The moment you accept another has some form of ability that is somehow lacking in yourself, you give the other authority over you, knowingly or in most cases unwittingly. Being fearful of those abilities is one thing, denying them as nothing is a whole other form of vulnerability waiting to happen!

The abilities that cause such a divisive response in most are in reality very natural aspects of our physiology; akin to experiencing temperature differences, sensing the mood of other people or the body's own ability to heal itself. The degree of sophistication with which your abilities in the area manifest themselves depends on a specific form of intelligence.

This intelligence can be measured, just as we measure academic intelligence (IQ), emotional intelligence (EQ), or sexual intelligence (XQ). The particular form of intelligence we shall be exploring in this Home Experience is Psychic Intelligence, which is quantified on a scale of PsyQ.

Traditionally, psychic or supernatural skills are focused on what is outside of us; leading us to the dark, unknown world where things lurk in the night. The study and development of your PsyQ shifts our attention inwards, to what we experience within ourselves.

Hence, when tapping into and leveraging your PsyQ, your main *tool* is you!

The way you work in any given environment or in your practice will dictate the quality of what you glean from your senses. How you experience and interpret this sensory information will influence the clarity and accuracy of the insight you have and feedback you can offer.

This Home Experience explores a collection of exercises you can use in your everyday life. These, combined with the philosophy behind our PsyQ development, form the basis for what others will say are superhuman gifts. This comes with a need for deep professionalism, whether or not you are working for yourself or professionally.

This approach will help you develop your body and mind's natural abilities to sense what is usually hidden, beyond the realms of normal perception. Once you start to develop your PsyQ, you will find a whole range of new and exciting activities is available to you.

These can include some of the practices covered in the Home Experience, but are not limited to these. Just as a person with a high IQ

can use their intelligence to pioneer new methods, a raised PsyQ will present you with opportunities you cannot read in books.

This introductory PsyQ Home Experience is the foundation level course that can lead you on to further training and professional PsyQ consultancy. Increasing your PsyQ will offer you many different abilities and new skills, many of which are equated with psychic mediums.

Over the next few weeks you will find yourself transitioning away from the traditional view of mediumship to focus upon the effect of a raised PsyQ. Rather than speculating upon what the results might mean, you will develop knowledge of yourself as a person and physiological being that far surpasses your accepted understanding.

Psychic mediums, be they naturally aware, self-taught or trained through an organisation or spiritualist church, tend to use a heightened PsyQ in a religious context. The PsyQ methodology nurtures us to the appreciation of our abilities (and what we interpret through using a high PsyQ) from a very different perspective.

You will learn to focus on the increase of PsyQ, keeping your attention facing inwards, instead of speculating upon concepts that are grounded in misguided, control-centric, fear-oriented beliefs. So, where a psychic medium will be interested in ghost and spirits, we are focused on fluid fields of vibration we sense in our bodies and the interpretation of these.

Fields of energy are very different to the way physical beings experience the world, so a true comprehension of energy requires quite a major shift in perception. We tend to separate things, to reduce things to make them simple and view experiences through time. In vibrational (or quantum) terms, space, time and separation are all illusions—side effects of the conscious, physical world.

To begin this process of recognising, experiencing and interpreting energy fields, we develop our sensory skills, so we can begin to interact with the vibrations that exist everywhere around and within us.

Developing your sensory abilities in order to perceive other levels and states of being can be an exciting and rewarding exercise, but increasing your PsyQ also requires regular practice and a commitment to evolve as a person in many ways. Whilst some people do retain varying degrees of PsyQ ability from childhood, most of us have to relearn how to use our additional sensory abilities.

PsyQ development is not really about *seeing ghosts*, although this is very often the aspect of it that catches the imagination. The ethos of both *Redefining Your PsyQ* and *Unleash Your PsyQ* seeks to create a degree of focus and determination not present in life for most.

People tend to be wanderers in life; travelling from path to path, place to place, without any overarching intent or plan. They are swayed by their desires, emotions and the way organisations leverage these. If we allow the next alluring thing to knock us off track, we will end up wandering through life, trying to get back to our life purpose.

Each of us has a life purpose that is absolutely unique to the individual person. Whether you believe in some meaningful master plan, a chaotic, unordered universe or anything in-between (or beyond), there is something in life that you can achieve, which no other person could do in the same way you do.

A developed PsyQ is one aspect of knowing this purpose in a profound way. When you have a palpable sense of your purpose, with all the nuance and depth you possess, you start experiencing the world differently.

You can use these experiences to sense what others do not; to know what they do not know and to see what most are blind to. The information you unlock within your body will translate into a contrasting view of the environment and the people or objects in it,

This empowers you to help people with therapeutic treatments, personal readings or sensing forces that exist beyond our comprehension or ability to quantify.

Very often the first step towards increasing your PsyQ is to leave behind any preconceived ideas about what you think is going to happen and begin practising techniques that sometimes appear to bear no relation to the end result!

PsyQ training can be compared to how operatic performers develop the ability to sing. This often means they do not sing for several months in favour of breathing exercises and abdominal crunches!

There are several steps in this initial PsyQ development process, each of which is listed here with a brief explanation of why we require it.

This initial stage of any PsyQ training process is integral to evolving yourself to the required level of sensory health. Good health is an important factor when employing the PsyQ because we are using the same system to sense vibrations as is used to coordinate your body's own healing response.

When interpreting your experiences, we need to piggy-back on the body-wide network that deals in analogue data—vibrations of energy. These are sensed from the environments we encounter and are usually very subtle. If your vibrational network is saturated with the strategic coordination of white-blood cell and platelet distribution, this will drown out the sensations you need.

If you have experienced trauma or emotional upheaval in your past, this can also hinder and even halt the ability to sense vibrational energy. We cannot connect to an experience and decipher the information it contains when swamped by the heaviness of fear, anger, grief, hatred, jealousy and so on. These emotions and their effect on our vibrational network stop us lifting the sensory experience to a level associated with the abilities we seek.

The more you can reduce any overpowering experience; softening the *traffic* through your vibrational network, the more you will perceive in your sensory work. The higher your PsyQ, the more you will be able to manoeuvre past any noise in your system; this does however take practice, time and real commitment to your craft.

Clearing and Healing

Raising your awareness of the vibrational fields you encounter could be viewed as an extension to the healing and clearing processes, as it continues to hone in upon the experience of your vibrational sensations. As you cast aside the ambient *noise* of contractive emotion and trauma, you elevate yourself to a place where you connect to vibrations that will assist in the development process.

To understand the processes of PsyQ development better we could use the analogy of a person trying to climb a cliff-face: the bottom is the starting point and the top is a state of proficiency in PsyQ ability.

Raised Awareness and Focus

They start up the cliff with a rucksack on their back that is filled with heavy pieces of rock. These could be seen as their contractive, painful emotions or trauma that constantly chatter in the vibrational network within us all. By dropping each rock in turn, they weigh less and climbing the cliff is easier.

Once they have dropped all the rocks, they can start to raise their awareness, which could be viewed as using helium-filled balloons to make them lighter. These balloons can actually lift our climber up so high that they no longer need to climb—they simply float upwards to their goal!

Another aspect of our training that goes hand in hand with the raising of awareness is that of focus. Without the ability to focus completely on our vibrational environment, we are often too distracted by other elements to glean any valuable information. Some people find the inability to focus on what they are doing so strong that it actually hinders their development and they give up trying.

Increased Sensitivity

Once you have honed to a deeper experience of the vibrational fields in your awareness, the next step is recognising that you have done so. This is another area where people often need help in their training, as preconceived ideas of what they should be *seeing* or *sensing* detract from what they are *actually* feeling.

The initial stages of your PsyQ growth may present you with what is known as *synaesthesia*—vague internal images, words, coloured light, faint smells or tastes, strange and indescribable feelings. These are all signs of the initial awakening within you as your senses try to find a means of translating the new information they are discovering.

How we sense vibrations around us depends on how we function as a person and, as we all work in a unique way, this means discovering your dominant senses and type of synaesthesia experiences. Some people lean towards a visual sense while others hear more. You may be a person who feels things or even works with smells and tastes!

Be aware that we have many more senses than the commonly-accepted five. You may experience results through the modality of these, which include electromagnetic senses, movement senses, temperature senses and so on.

Once you know what your main sensory avenue is, the most conducive method of learning is to concentrate on that sense and move your main focus away from the other senses. Very often people want to *see* so much that they ignore the very loud messages they are *hearing*, whereas if they were to concentrate on experiencing those aural messages they would eventually start to sense changes in vibration visually in addition to the audio.

Intuitive Ability

Your intuition can be described as the way you interpret the information you have recognised, via your senses. The interpretation you glean on each occasion will depend on how you process the world around you and bring together all that you have learnt, with whatever perceptual biases you current have.

So, having recognised the subtle information in your environment, you need to understand it in some way. Your intuitive skills will enable you to do this, translating vibrations into usable concepts, based on your worldview, which you can then communicate to others or use as an insight into the environment around you.

Imagination and Descriptive Skills

These skills are another interesting, yet often underrated, aspect of PsyQ development as we usually try to divorce the experiences of PsyQ from those of our imagination. One of the most common pieces of feedback given by an adventurer who is starting the journey in the realms of PsyQ is, "But did I imagine it?"

The honest answer... Yes, you did!

You are picking up on physical, very real vibrations of energy in your immediate surroundings and mapping these through your body, emotions and mind. You are then recognising these vibrations and interpreting them.

Now, while your senses will provide an accurate picture of what is there, it falls to your imagination to translate what you feel. The part of your brain that deals with translation of vibrational information is also the part that drives your imagination—so in the initial stages of training it does seem like you are imagining it!

However, as we progress and experience more and more, we learn to decipher what is *translation* and what is *creation*. We know *this* is PsyQ information and *that* is what we have made up. It is only with evolution, practice and a belief in yourself that this differentiation comes, but with time and perseverance it will happen.

The flip side of this is, once you have a workable translation of what you have experienced, how do you convey this to others?

It is surprising how difficult it can be to communicate what we perceive in a way that expresses exactly what we feel and imparts the intricacies of our experiences. Very often it is inadequate descriptive skills that let us down, so expansion of our illustrative skills is also a crucial element of PsyQ ability.

Those who are unprepared to develop a rich and diverse way of communication that accurately captures their experiences, revert to the common themes that plague this area of human experience. It is so easy to simply talk in terms of established belief systems that are dogmatic, reductive and open you up to scepticism.

Assertion and Confidence

The final phase in this introductory journey of PsyQ training is that of assertion and confidence which we could view as *knowing oneself*. By gathering an in-depth knowledge of yourself and who you are, you will trust yourself with greater integrity. This degree of confidence in yourself also helps you to become unsusceptible to *external influence* which, contrary to popular belief, is human in origin rather than paranormal!

Assertion is traditionally known as *protection*, but for specific reasons, it is imperative to use the term *assertion*. By asserting yourself, you will be less likely to undergo entrainment from the vibrations you connect to and can therefore make the conscious decision as to whether the vibrations you are dealing with are conducive for you.

Assertion enables you to interact with energy fields and develop your PsyQ in a way that is beneficial, empowering and comfortable for you.

Confidence is derived from your assertion; the more assertive you are, the more confident you will feel. Confidence is vital to the leveraging of PsyQ ability. We need confidence in ourselves and in the information we get, as well as the confidence to express that information.

By developing your confidence, you support your PsyQ, plus you evolve in personality and strength of character. The important thing to remember with confidence is not to let it develop into *arrogance* or allow it to be dented by the arrogance of others.

Confidence is a belief in yourself, whereas arrogance is a belief that you are better than others at something. We need confidence to work with our PsyQ, but this can have a tendency to develop into the arrogance of believing that we are right and others are wrong.

We all work in our own, unique ways and have different experiences of the vibrations around us. When we sense something differently to another person, the idea is to develop the confidence to believe in what you find for yourself while understanding that the other person's interpretation is equally valid.

We should also be aware that if another tells us that they are right and we are wrong, we should be confident enough to stand firm in our abilities and not permit them to dent our belief in those abilities and skills.

The First Few Steps

As you embark on this Home Experience, you will have your own opinions and beliefs about what PsyQ ability is and how it feels to increase PsyQ. Part of the initial purpose of this path is to break down the old viewpoints that are based in the art of control and superiority.

By discovering a different method of discovering and enhancing your abilities, you can develop a new way of sensing the world around you. By shifting your perspective, removing any misconceptions and changing the methods you use to hone your abilities, you will soon see a major improvement in your experiential ability.

The techniques and training tools you will encounter on this journey are unlike anything that has gone before and will help you to become more than you ever imagined in very tangible ways.

The traditional focus of psychic development lies in areas such as attending circle, practising meditation and creating protection. However in this Home Experience we shall shift the emphasis to a change of perspective.

PsyQ is a measure of something within us all. The only reason you may have not be aware of this in yourself or have found your PsyQ to be low, is because you have not known where to look, your health needs improvement or some trauma from your past is blocking you from progressing.

Once you modify your perception to a place where you are able to read and understand the information offered by your PsyQ experiences, you will find that your skills light up and start blossoming.

Some people who venture upon this path will already have worked on attaining a high PsyQ and are either unaware of how they can hone their abilities or are frightened by them. Others may want a form of qualification or formal training for professional use and some may want to learn simply what to do with their skills or discover some of the specialist traits of a high PsyQ.

Whatever your reasons for being here, it is safe to assume that your commitment is beyond that of a taster workshop or quick-fix weekend. The path of this journey will reflect this power and depth of knowledge—the wisdom you will encounter is aimed at assisting you to a level where you can use your skills in a professional arena.

It is due to the professional nature of the qualification this path leads to that we investigate the theoretical, philosophical and scientific topics in such depth. This knowledge will ensure your abilities, not only in PsyQ development, but also in the realms of insurance, employment and the law.

So, it is with great excitement and many good wishes that you are invited to venture forward to the great wonderment and deeply profound experiences of PsyQ. Enjoy every moment, for you are becoming the person you are destined to be, gaining greater insights into your world and yourself with each and every step of the journey.

An Unconventional Learning Experience

This Home Experience is sculpted using an integrated system of printed learning materials, practical techniques, vibrational and subliminal information as well as a digital realm, which adds a rich media experience to your learning journey.

The very nature of PsyQ development means that you are working on levels of your psyche other than conscious thought. Dedicating a significant part of the journey towards your subconscious development makes the learning more effective and easier.

Honouring the development of your own PsyQ and how this will benefit you and others, are at the core of the Home Experience ethos. With the recognition that a change in perception requires the integration of both your subconscious and consciousness, in order to produce the desired results, we seek to layer the learning experience over many different areas of your psyche.

It is vital to work through each element, without relying on a favoured style or method of learning. Some prefer reading printed books to exploring online, others prefer watching videos to text and so on. The transmedia structure of this experience is sculpted in such a way, that missing one layer can cause you to miss out on an important aspect of the whole journey.

The contrasting methods used to do this can be divided up like this:

Practical—Physical, Chemical, Sensory

(Physically based exercises)

- Various PsyQ-increasing techniques
- Various practical sessions
- Arena environments
- Sensory and muscle memory exercises

Subliminal—Lower Cerebral
(Subconscious Study)

- Sub-aural and binaural audio
- Linguistic triggers and Viridia Lingua
- Autogenic entrainment

Cerebral—Conscious Thought
(Thought orientated study)

- Printed course materials
- Digital experiences and resources
- Journalling

Energetic Information—Higher Cerebral

- Orientations and Calibrations
- Click Track learning
- Vibrationally encoded materials
- Synaesthesia enhancement

Spiritual/Inter-dimensional—Beyond Perception

- vState entrainment
- Vibrational cognition and interaction
- Legacy creation

Vibrationally Encoded Notes

One of the main principles of vibrational energy is that it does not adhere to the artificial concepts of space and time. Relativity Theory hypothesises that for an object, travelling from one place to another, time will slow down the closer it gets to the speed of light.

Hence, a beam of light travels so fast that time literally stops—there is no time.

Imagine for a moment that you are a beam of light travelling across the vast reaches of space. If there is no time, how long does it take you to travel two miles? A hundred miles? A million miles?

Well, it takes you no time at all—from your perspective as this beam of light, the journey is instantaneous. If you can travel two or two million miles in an instant, how do you measure space?

In the same moment you can travel anywhere, so all space exists in the same moment. If here, there and everywhere all exist concurrently in your consciousness, how do you quantify or measure where you are?

You are literally everywhere in that one moment! If you were a beam of light, you would never grow a single second older and everything you have ever done or will do happens in the blink of an eye.

Now from our human perspective, light travelling from one place to another does take time (because we are not travelling as fast as light). For example, a ray of light emitted from the sun takes eight minutes to get to Earth. Light travelling from Barnard's Star, our sun's closest neighbour, takes two light years.

So, from where we are standing, light does take time to travel from place to place, thus must be affected by time, surely? Remember that the only reason light appears to adhere to the concepts of time and space is because it is travelling at the speed of light and we are not!

This demonstrates that whilst we perceive a concept in one way, perception is relative and things are not always as they seem.

Vibrations or quanta of energy follow this same principle, existing outside of space and time and thus, when you interact with vibrations of energy, we hook into that same timelessness. This very fact means that we can leverage energy in fantastic ways, via a means of vibrational encoding.

To appreciate how this works, it is important to recognise the encoding is not a physical thing—this book is not printed technologically advanced paper, nor does it use special, vibrational ink! Instead, we use the concept of *energy beyond space and time* to establish a parallel between the encode and your experience.

In the methodology of One Therapy, we use orientations and calibrations, where a student experiences a pre-defined orientation (range of vibrations), through a process of Calibration. The vibrational encoding is similar to this inasmuch as the materials found in this Home Experience have specific vibrations of energy associated with them.

Some of these vibrations will help sensitise you to work better with the techniques we cover on the way, whilst the others are adaptable and *record* the vibrational shift events of your practice experiences.

Here, the practice experiences you have are captured, rather like a vibrational photograph—these exist both in the instant you conducted the practice and every instance you *replay the recording* (in energetic terms these are the same moment and spatial environment). So, whenever you trigger the vibrational recording you relive the moment vibrationally again.

In human terms, you will experience these moment, weeks, months, maybe years apart, however the vibrations simply exist. The powerful aspect of this process is that each time you trigger a recording, you experience it from your evolved, learned perspective— this results in sensations and synaesthesia you have not experienced before.

As all vibrational encodes are consciously sensed and interpreted in the moment if you missed something first time around, as soon as you have developed your PsyQ to the degree where you can actually interpret that level vibration, it is there to be triggered.

The main purpose of encoding is so you can experience and relive the things that cannot be written on these pages: your experiences. Whether it is your personal calibration to an orientation, the sensations of the practical exercises or the answers to questions that you asked—yes, even these can be vibrationally attached so that you remind yourself of the answers.

The triggering of a recording or pre-defined vibrational range is very simple to initiate... by using a finger on the relevant encode trigger—these can be found on each page. Placing your finger in the appropriate place does not create a physical reaction—it does not activate that non-existent, technologically advanced paper or special ink—it is a statement of intent.

The results are sensory and synaesthesia-based, therefore, when you place your finger on the encode trigger of a particular page, you are stating that you want to trigger any *recordings* associated with the content of that page.

Go ahead, try it here... place a finger on the encode trigger image and then sit quietly, breathing slowly and allow yourself to open up to the internal experiences that follow.

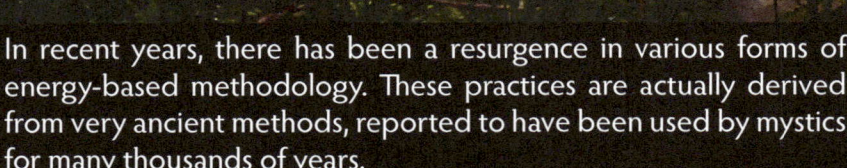

Orientation and Calibration

In recent years, there has been a resurgence in various forms of energy-based methodology. These practices are actually derived from very ancient methods, reported to have been used by mystics for many thousands of years.

The traditional context of these arts are as a lifelong endeavours, where the practitioner invests many hours every day to enhance their experience of energy. These forces, known as Ki, Chi, Prana and so on, are mystical powers that interact with the body, mind and spirit to create holistic wellbeing.

In modern terms, these ancient traditions are still used; however a new breed of practitioners cannot spare the many hours needed each day to master their art. Instead, systems of attunement or empowerment enable a master to teach their student the experience of universal forces.

Various ways of training people how to work with vibrational practices have been developed—in the context of this Home Experience, the method of learning how to sense vibrations using a heightened degree of PsyQ is twofold.

The first stage is known as *orientation*, where the PsyQ Master conducts a specific range of techniques in preparation for the second aspect of the process; the *calibration*. Orientations work by calming the mind sufficiently enough to distinguish subtle vibrational information and by boosting the amplitude of vibrational waves to make them easier to recognise.

The calibration process is not simply recognising the vibrations, but creating profound adaptations to the way you experience vibrations. Using your body as an antenna and your mind as a way of recognising and interpreting the messages received by that antenna, you calibrate over time.

The orientation and calibration system is still a relatively mysterious process that has very little basis in science—we are still unable to say with any definitive idea what is actually happening.

Sceptics view the more widely known *attunement* process found in Reiki modalities as pseudoscience or placebo. This reaction usually stems from the philosophy of attunements—one that is steeped in mysticism and spiritual beliefs.

Here, for the purposes of our PsyQ enhancement, we could view the process of orientation and calibration to be a simple case of transference or entrainment, albeit transpersonal in nature.

We can say that orientations and calibrations work very successfully, whether the person calibrating believes or not. Millions of people across the globe, in various different practices all speak in testament to the efficacy of these forms of knowledge-transmission. Whether there is a mystical reason, a scientific one, or it is all placebo—it works!

The frequencies of vibrational energy experienced in calibration are specific to the results required and every orientation you experience in this Home Experience is tailored to your specific needs at the time.

To appreciate what is happening in the calibration to an orientation, imagine that you were speaking to somebody who had never seen the colour blue—how would you describe this to them, so that they could understand what you mean? It is impossible without a point of reference!

However, if you could show them a piece of blue-coloured paper, they would instantly know what blue is and they would never forget it. This is the equivalent of the orientation and calibration experience—the master demonstrates the specific vibrations of that orientation and the adventurer instantly experiences those vibrations through the calibrations they conduct over time.

The vibrations you experience in each orientation and calibration will never be forgotten and can always be used, even if you have not practised for many years. The understanding of each orientation does take a while to integrate fully with your system. So you may notice that the effects increase with time, becoming stronger certainly over the three weeks after the initial calibration.

Of course, the more you work with the different vibrations of energy, the better you will understand them and the results you will obtain will be greater (and faster).

Over time you may notice some strange sensory experiences related to the orientation and calibration as conscious knowledge of the vibrations affect your experiences, thus helping you develop your skills.

The reason you experience these changes is your brain trying to understand the increased volume in analogue (vibrational), data, facilitated by your growing PsyQ. Until you learn to consciously recognise this information in your own way, your brain translates the *messages* as it would the information provided by your other senses—we call this *mapping* of sensory experience *synaesthesia*.

These synaesthesia may involve any sensory experience, from sight, hearing, taste and smell to the various motion and kinaesthetic senses that we feel. Common effects include:

Brightly coloured flashes of light

Strobe effects

Shapes and movement in front of the eyes

Distortions
(such as that caused by looking through heat)

High-pitched tones/tinnitus

Rapid tapping inside the ear
(as if a moth is flying about inside)

Inexplicable smells/perfumes
(that last only for a moment)

Peculiar tastes in your mouth

Strange feelings of emotion

Emotional outbursts

Tingling
(especially in the head, hands and feet)

Headaches

Cold/flu-like symptoms

Extremes of heat and cold

Magnetic pulling/pushing in hands or body

Vibrations/trembling sensations
(especially in the spine)

The feeling of being touched or prodded

Imagery and visions

Sensing a presence in the room

Random words or thoughts that stand out

When your PsyQ
is not at a sufficient
level, vibrations
and the information
encapsulated within,
will pass you by.

When you have developed
your PsyQ, vibrational
information can be sensed
and interpreted through the
experience of synaesthesia.

These are just some of the sensory experiences you may find immediately after calibration; however do not be surprised if you have other effects not mentioned here. These are all natural processes and are in no way detrimental to you.

The more unpleasant side effects will clear, becoming easier over time. They will disappear once you have integrated the orientation. Beyond the maximum of a three-week detox, you will notice increased synaesthesia, which becomes stronger over time.

In some instances, people also report increased dream activity and EHS (Exploding Head Syndrome), where loud noises, voices and other high volume sounds are heard when dropping off to sleep.

These are all part of increased PsyQ and, whilst somewhat disconcerting at first, will become a profound, glorious part of your heightened awareness. It is important to focus on the internal experience of synaesthesia, rather than projecting dogmatic tradition onto your experiences.

So, if you see a visual disturbance or feel as if you are being touched, direct your thoughts to the synaesthesia itself and not to *there is something there* or *somebody is touching me*.

The reasons for this will become apparent in time; for now, however, understand how concentrating on your internal experience empowers you, asserts your will and is a testament to your PsyQ abilities. Externalising experiences into the outside world, disempowers, increases feelings of vulnerability and can induce unwanted emotions.

Click-Track Learning

In addition to the encoded materials, orientations and calibrations encountered in this Home Experience, there are additional methods of learning available, which revolutionise your journey.

Developed especially for PsyQ training, *Click-Track* systems are in place to ensure that you are constantly evolving your degree of PsyQ. Each click track consists of a band of specific vibrations that work on a cycle (this is the *track*).

During this cycle there may be various points at which the cycle stops and works with particular facets of your being, perhaps to heal a trauma or to boost the sensitivity of a specific part of you (these stopping points are the *clicks*).

At the beginning of our journey together, with the first calibration, you connect into the start of the click track and your vibrational physiology (along with other cerebral and physiological systems) are developed in parallel with the track. Hence, your experience evolves with each click that is passed.

Once the cycle is completed, it begins again, but this time from a different perspective. So what appears to be a continuous circle of experiences, is actually a spiral that will enable you to advance your skills for the entire length of the course.

Thus, a click track acts as a single cycle from the start to a desired result. Here, the energetic vibrations repeat over and over again. Once you connect to the vibrations of the click track at the beginning of the Home Experience and with each repetition, expand your awareness so that by the end of the adventure you have spiralled your abilities beyond what they were before.

A Click Track simply repeats itself...

Click

The Vibrational *Track*

With every repetition, the Click Track expands your awareness, creating a spiral effect.

Arena Environment

The Arena Environment methodology was also created for PsyQ development, using techniques available in the Viridian Method; due to its success in the testing phase. Arenas are now also used extensively throughout One Therapy modalities for teaching purposes.

The Arenas implemented here are twofold— the first Arena is set up as part of the classroom each time you are exploring the realms and the second is your personal Arena. This is an environment for you to transition into for personal practice and encounters.

Arenas work by *emulating* a particular type of environment, for example, an environment conducive to learning.

Let us imagine that you are walking into a room, such as your living room at home. As you enter, you instinctively connect to the ambient energy of the room and will recognise this as being *s*.

When you walk into the room of an eighteenth-century mansion, the same thing happens, except here you may choose to connect to the ambient vibrations associated with the moment you enter the room or the vibrational profile of the room in 1746!

Certainly, if the events of 1746 leave a stronger vibrational imprint on the room's ambience than the vibrations of today, you are more likely to sense the experience of those events.

In every moment we are presented with choices, with layers of vibrational energy we can decide between. You could connect into the experience of 1746 in your living room, but it is most likely that the vibrations of your personal experience in the room will be stronger.

This is why people often remark that they feel sixteen again, when returning to the parental home or why some pick up on emotions in a room, whilst others do not. We can actually connect into far more than we have ever imagined. You could connect to the experience of your living room, whilst in the room of the eighteenth-century mansion, if you so desired!

We naturally, automatically connect into the strongest ambience of a room, but we can work with an infinite array of vibrational perspectives, just by connecting into the layer of our choosing. That layer creates a multidimensional experience in our physical environment to distract our conscious awareness away from the ambient and towards the desired.

This is how an Arena works—you connect to a place where your ability to learn is enhanced, along with feelings of confidence, nurture and security. In this Arena your skills will be increased and you will feel totally at ease. This is a safe place where you can practise your abilities and increase your PsyQ, so that when you transfer these skills into the ambient environment they will be equally effective.

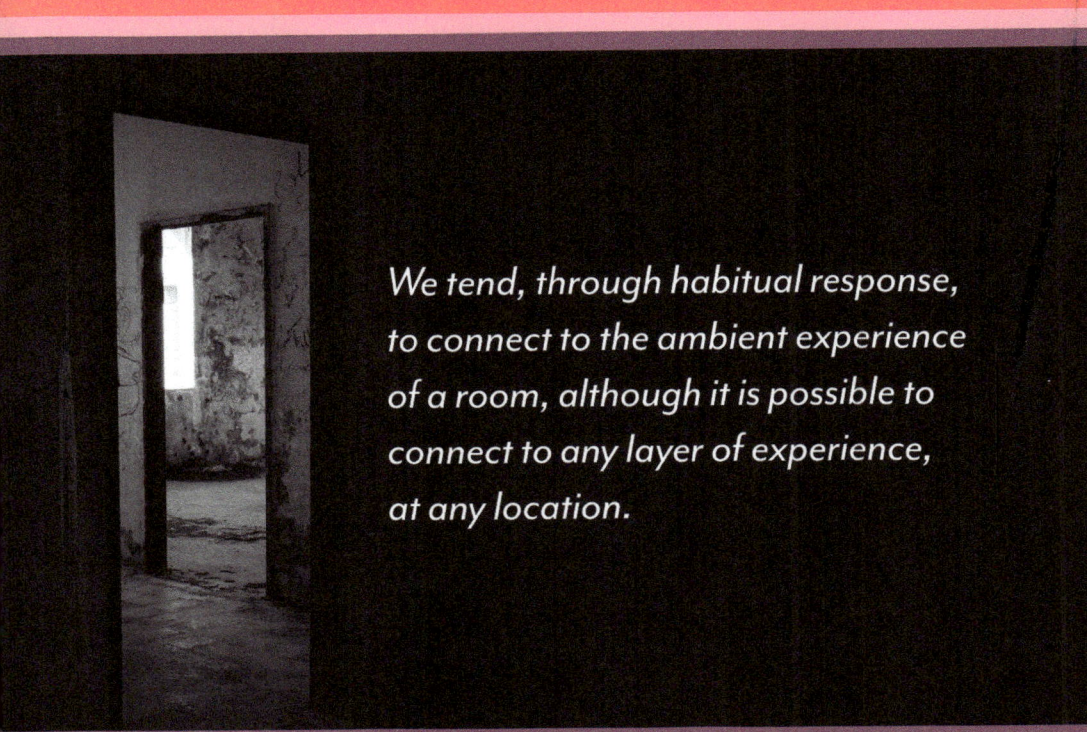

We tend, through habitual response, to connect to the ambient experience of a room, although it is possible to connect to any layer of experience, at any location.

*The Arena creates a neutral environment
we can use for many purposes,
including increasing PsyQ and learning
how to use this for a variety of results.*

Both Arena Environments (the realm and your Personal Arenas) are available to you now and will continue throughout your Home Experience adventures. These will also come with Arena entities, which are very special intelligences—they will guide and help you throughout your development. We shall look at these entities later on the journey and how to work with them to greater degrees.

The PsyQ Experience

The shadow-soaked figure stands in a patch of dense thicket, watching. He is silent and still. His eyes are fixed and focused on something in the distance, although he sees nothing except the surrounding trees.

In the dark, half-light of evening, he stands; a sentinel, seeking sanctuary in the forest… his body painted to camouflage him from the dangers that lurk here. He has spent his short life alone; only just a teenager, yet fending for himself in a very different world to our own.

Here, humans are hunters and hunted… by the creatures that share their world and by each other. The threat of injury or death is palpable in every moment, dispelling any hope of sleep or the briefest rest.

The darkness was especially terrifying—the risks were greater; the visceral fear more overwhelming. Yet, he stood defiant against the night, the darkness and the fear. Sheltered by the cloak of shadow and thick undergrowth, he knew there were creatures here with much better sight than him. To them, this darkness did not obscure their prey… and he was their prey.

This tall, brave boy, who was an adult despite his minute experience of life, breathed slow and shallow. He knew something was out there in the blackness—something that meant to kill him. It had been stalking him for a while and he knew this from the very instant the beast became aware of him.

He had not seen the creature. Neither heard, smelt or felt it. But every fibre of his being knew it was out there. He understood what the creature was, its location and hunting pattern. He would recognise every change of pace and movement. And he would experience the attack, the moment it started… even though it would come from an enormous distance.

This lonely human watched and waited; and the darkness closed in.

To survive, our early ancestors needed a set of innate skills that we have forgotten over time. They needed to evade life-threatening dangers in the night; to sense what our modern-day senses could not sense until it was too late.

They needed to hunt; to attain enough food to survive and to outwit creatures, sensitive to the slightest sound or movement. Early humans needed to experience the world differently to us... and they needed to possess skills that we cannot even comprehend.

Our ancestors demonstrated skills that are derived from a high PsyQ.

In modern society, when a person claims to sense something that cannot be seen, heard or felt, they are labelled delusional or revered as gurus. However, we all have the ability to achieve remarkable abilities that defy the cold rational logic of our twenty-first century.

These strange and powerful senses have simply become atrophied over time; rarely used as we learned to adapt our environment around us, rather than matching the specific nature of our surroundings. There is nothing mysterious or special about these abilities, once the deception of time is removed from the picture.

In our contemporary perspective; overwhelmed and reductive, we assume that our ancestors were just like us—except shorter and with very limited lifespans. However, they experienced the world around them in a very different way. They needed to be a part of the world and in their environment, rather than focusing on dogmatic and pragmatic thought constructs.

When using your PsyQ you will gain the ability to sense vibrations of energy that are usually not perceived in conscious perception. We can sense high frequency/high amplitude energy, such as sunlight or music, but we do not usually sense extremely low-frequency (ELF) Energy.

Everybody can interpret ELF by
boosting the power (amplitude)
of the energy and discovering/
honing their senses to it.
There are specific vibrations
of energy that are associated
with a healthy degree of PsyQ
and we can call these the layers
of psychic perception.

We are constantly aware of these
vibrations—we just do not realise it!
The more you hone your ability to
consciously decipher what you
sense around you, the greater
your PsyQ will be. Remember,
at all times, what you decipher
from your subtle senses is unique
to your individual perspective
and therefore, individual to you.

We tend to express intelligence in terms of IQ (Intelligence Quotient), which focuses upon how effectively we process information, our academic skills and education—basically, how *clever* we are. Yet, there are many other forms of intelligence, beyond the left-brain, cerebral function.

Emotional intelligence (EQ), spiritual intelligence (SQ) and behavioural intelligence (BQ) are three examples. Here, we seek to explore and grow our PsyQ: the intelligence of our psyche and higher psychological perception. Our ancestors had a high PsyQ; essential to their survival and the reason they became so effective at evolving in extraordinary ways.

Our evolution, cultural and social, has shifted how we perceive our world from PsyQ to IQ. The result—a world of memes and beliefs that disconnect us from our instinct, intuition and knowing. What many might refer to as our psychic abilities.

Most people have their own, very distinct and personal opinions on what *being psychic* is all about. The challenge is, these opinions are usually engrained within an obsolete tradition that is not wholly true (and certainly not beneficial in our modern world).

A common inaccuracy is that being psychic is a gift, whilst another initial misconception is that we use psychic abilities to look out there for the experiences we require. Both of these beliefs exist before we even get to how we define experiences, once we have them.

In the West, anything vaguely psychic is immediately processed through the philosophies of many religions, usually the Judaeo-Christian perspective. The terminology and imagery here ranges from the emotionally profound to the downright terrifying. The notion of demons, ghosts, spirits and angels are the *must-have items* for any psychic medium.

However, what happens when we strip away the theology and tradition, in favour of a very different way of understanding the psychic phenomena? What can we experience and achieve when we rewrite an ability as a form of intelligence? What if we understand being psychic, not as a ghost hunter or fortune teller, but as a person leveraging an innate and powerful sensory experience?

The aptitude to tap into our PsyQ can be traced specifically to a person's capacity to sense the information that travels through a particular part of the nervous system. People who learn how to consciously recognise this information show enhanced intuitive/sensitive abilities. Hence, each and every person with a healthy nervous system can discover their psychic sense, by looking inwards to what their body offers them.

We could expand upon this idea by comparing the use of PsyQ with that of a TV set. All around us (and within us) are complex fields of energy that exist at every single point of the universe. Whilst not as widespread, we can compare the broadcasts of television transmissions to this energy. Your TV uses a receiver to pick up on these transmissions, which are then decoded as images and sounds.

The vibrational information we use when working with PsyQ, exists as part of this omnipresent energy, however it is our nervous system that acts as the receiver and the brain which decodes the information (the TV set).

When sitting down of an evening to watch your favourite programme, you do not stare at the walls, through which the transmissions are travelling or through the window in the direction of the transmitter. You watch the screen of the TV set. The process is the same to access your PsyQ and sense the information it possesses.

Now just as different people enjoy different programmes on TV or dislike TV altogether, information received through a healthy PsyQ relies on the same principle of perspective. Imagine that you are walking down the street and see a friend across the road; you may think that what you are seeing is *real*, but it is not!

What you are actually seeing relies on factors such as your ability to assess distances, your spatial awareness and how your brain translates the information from your senses (in this example, your eyes). We often think that seeing is believing, but the things we see are merely our perspective—what is actually there is often very different.

Essentially, in this example, energy (in the form of light) is bouncing off your friend, across the road to your eye. The eye then sends information about this energy to the brain for decoding. Depending on the way your eye receives the information and how your brain translates it, you will see something that is unique to you.

So people will often perceive things differently from each other, based upon factors such as colour-perception, cultural upbringing and psychological function. The same is true for the information that you sense through your PsyQ—what you are seeing, hearing or feeling is not *out there*, it is inside of you and depends heavily on how you perceive the world around you.

If you can master the internal reception and translation of the vibrational data, you will refine your skills and hone your abilities. It is imperative to this process however, that you understand it is the internal workings of your body—not the source of what you perceive.

Of course, the stronger any energetic source is and the better versed you are at translating that source, the greater the results you will achieve. Traditionally, in Western culture, people practise by sitting *in circle* and while it is not imperative to work in a group, regular practice is vital to your progress. Those who practise their development techniques each and every day tend to advance much quicker than those who work sporadically.

Two other cornerstones that will help practice are firstly, to be open minded to whatever you experience—we are used to ignoring our PsyQ, so it has to work in rather *interesting* ways to get our attention, particularly in the preliminary stages of development training. For the second cornerstone, concentrate on what you *are* getting, rather than what you are *not* getting! Some people often sabotage their psychic development by focusing on what other people experienced and not what they have achieved themselves, albeit in different areas.

In the first few stages of developing your PsyQ, you may find that information comes as thoughts, mental images, physical sensations (touching, being pulled/pushed), tones or tapping in the ears, lights/ shadows and so on. As you progress and particularly, as you focus on enhancing your personal skills, you will find that these subtle experiences become more tangible and definite. Your brain is simply learning to interpret the information it is receiving and the more you allow it to do so, the more confident you will become.

Another misconception about being psychic is what we actually do with our abilities. People often associate psychic mediums either with ghosts or crystal balls—and while both the paranormal and personal readings do comprise a large part of psychic ability work, a high PsyQ will assist you in many other fields of interest, such as questing, psychometry, healing therapies and higher cerebral activities, such as remote viewing, astral travel, environmental entrainment, inter-dimensional communication and so on.

The art of our PsyQ is to perceive that which is usually imperceivable and to experience realms that lie beyond experience. We glean that which is not consciously known to us (and, on occasion, other people) so that it benefits those who ask us for help. We are also in the business of healing, both ourselves and others—everything you do using PsyQ will impact your holistic health—so always remember to act in a professional and compassionate manner.

Contrasting Perspectives

Physiological Perception (including EQ)

Intellectual Perception (IQ)

Psychic Perception (PsyQ)

Transpersonal Perception

Spiritual Perception (SQ)

Harnessing your PsyQ is not about achieving some mysterious power that we know very little about. A lot of scientific research has investigated the ways people function on a physiological level when working with their PsyQ abilities. It is frequently the case that people dislike such a seemingly mundane view of what some people believe is a very special gift.

However, by removing the mystery and dispelling the clandestine nature of our PsyQ, we actually see the true gifts that exist beyond the physical (the aspects of our PsyQ that cannot be measured or quantified).

All we need to do is recognise that we are using different parts of our anatomy from those we usually pay attention to and this shift of perception offers immense wonderment.

If it is just a simple shift of perception that is required to develop your psychic abilities, why do some people have such difficulty in creating this shift and why are we not all using these abilities as second nature?

The reason is twofold.

Initially, there are aspects of ourselves that block our perception of the vibrational information we perceive and secondly, the fact that we do not recognise our subtle senses, means these become atrophied over time and thus, harder to perceive. Therefore, to attain this shift in perception it is necessary to work with two different approaches. The first is to remove any factors that hinder us and the second is to boost the sensory information that is the foundation of our vibrational awareness.

We can view our perception as a sphere with many layers—the more we expand our perception, the broader the array of abilities we obtain and the greater depth of experiences we achieve. For example, our vibrational perception exists beyond our usual cerebral perception, so we require an expansion of our perspective to reach it.

Everything we perceive in life can be represented as a sphere; the further we expand this sphere, the more we learn to perceive. As we expand our sphere on one level, all the other layers expand also, meaning that if your sphere of perception currently borders on cerebral perception (what you think), expanding it will cause your physical perception to

"It's dangerous!"

"I'm frightened of the unknown!"

"You Idiot! You'll never achieve anything!"

"Ghosts and Demons and Monsters, Oh My!"

"I always fail!"

"You need to protect yourself!"

"It's a gift, only meant for a few!"

"Don't meddle in things you know nothing about!"

also move towards the outer layers of the sphere. This is why we start recognising our vibrational information as intuitive thoughts and then develop stronger physical responses with time and practice.

In the PsyQ Home Experience, we are seeking to expand your sphere of perception as much as possible. The more you boost the potency of the outer layers, the easier they are to *find*. Plus, the more we can remove limitations to our expansion the smoother the process will be.

The limiting beliefs that you have been presented with by others in the past, will work against your efforts to expand your sphere, if you let them. Often you will have subconsciously taken these limiting beliefs as truth and actually believe them to be fact. So removing these limits, along with any other potential limitations, is an important step in your psychic development.

The more extensive your work on your subliminal limitations, the more expansive your perception will become. Here we shall look at five different approaches to assist this process of clearing limiting beliefs and boosting our energetic abilities. These five separate layers are:

- Holistic healing of the physical body, emotions and mind
- Repatterning subconscious habits
- Automatic entrainment
- Altering perception
- Vibrational mastership

The combination of techniques and exercises we shall be using to span these different layers, will work both on the change in perception, as well as boosting the information that is available to you.

Holistic Healing of the Physical Body, Emotions and Mind

On this adventure, we shall discover that the health of our physical body is intrinsically linked to the degree of our PsyQ because, not only do we require expansion of our physical layers to achieve the outer layers of our perspective sphere, but also when our bodies are preoccupied with healing, our PsyQ can be blocked out.

Our physical body not only includes the flesh, bones, blood, etc., as we also include the chemical reactions that occur bodywide (emotions) and the electrical transmissions in the brain (thoughts). These levels are integrally connected and by working on one level, you will have an effect on all three layers and beyond.

Repatterning Subconscious Habits

One of the most seemingly innocuous factors in PsyQ development turns out to be one of the most vital areas of attention. The habitual attachments we have to words and phrases. From birth, we are exposed to language as our main form of conscious communication and soon begin to form connections between the words we use and physiological reactions in the body.

Words such as *pain*, *hurt*, *anger*, *hatred*, *murder*, *abuse* and so on, quickly become associated with pain reactions at a chemical level. It is these pain reactions that soon start to sabotage our best efforts to achieve our a greater PsyQ. Partly as a result of limiting beliefs, but also due to emotional reactions we have to concepts subliminally attached to certain words.

By changing the linguistic approach we take towards PsyQ development, we change the chemical reactions in our body and thus, change our body and mind. This is the core belief of therapies such as NLP (Neuro-Linguistic Programming) and CWT (Creative Writing Therapy).

When we turn our attention to the intermediate techniques of our journey and experience the deep level meditations, altered awareness and trance-state tools of PsyQ methodology, it is helpful to place triggers at a subconscious level, as these will help us not only to activate the different techniques, but also to deactivate them!

We can also use other forms of *trigger* device, such as words or images, when working with vibrational elements of the Home Experience. For instance the *barcode* system of this adventure can be seen as an automatic entrainment trigger.

Automatic Entrainment

Altering Perception

The ability to alter your perception of the world will make the processes of development much easier and enable you to look beyond yourself, to a realm of fantastic wonders. As you shift your viewpoint, you will learn many wise lessons and obtain information that you could never understand from your *everyday* view of the world.

So if you perceive something that is blocking your progress and you are unable to move beyond this limitation, simply alter your perception to a place where the block no longer exists!

Vibrational Mastership

The vibrational elements of this course are something that over the past few years have become very popular, much talked about and to a certain extent placed into the realms of inaccuracy and dogma. Energy fields and the vibrational mastership that comes from knowing these, will help you when working with others. Your mastery will also enable you to perceive the world differently—from the viewpoint of energy!

Many of the PsyQ techniques have been developed specifically for the purposes of PsyQ development and cannot be found in any other learning programme.

Discovering Energy Fields and Their Vibrational Spectrum

Energy is a term that is used rather avidly these days. Exciting new developments in holistic medicine, science and self-development methods all use the basis: *everything in existence is created from energy*. Hence, we are beginning to understand the importance of energy to our very existence and especially in the realms of PsyQ and therapy work, where the foundations are deeply rooted in energetic philosophy.

The issue here is that many people who use the word *energy* do not actually understand what they are referring to when they use the term and have even less comprehension of how energy works.

Energy is force. It is the force to create a number of things such as heat or light or the power to generate movement. We can often sense the various effects of energy, such as seeing the light cast from a bulb, feeling the heat from a flame or the renewed vigour we get from eating a bar of chocolate.

amplitude

wavelength

wavelength per second = hertz (Hz)

Energy exists in small packets, known as *quanta*, which travel from one place to another by forming waves, rather like those seen on the ocean. These waves can be measured, in *wavelength* (the distance along the wave through one *trough* and one *peak*) and *amplitude* (the distance in height between a trough and a peak).

The number of peaks and troughs that travel through any given point in one second (cycles per second) is known as the frequency of a wave and is measured in hertz (Hz). The different frequencies and amplitudes of energy waveforms influence the effects they have.

For example, green light has a frequency of approximately 564 trillion cycles per second—if you increase the amplitude, the brighter the light will become, but if you change the frequency, you change the colour of the light.

This translates to the higher the frequency, the faster the quanta are travelling and the larger the amplitude the more quanta there are. In any given waveform, there can be any number of changes in frequency and amplitude and these changes are called modulation.

We modulate the sound waves that are created by our vocal cords in order to form words and therefore communicate through speech. We can also say that modulation in any form of energy can potentially communicate information.

So, we could look at green light and say that the information contained within that energy is that it has "this much brightness/power" and "564 trillion Hz". Wonderful—but what is the value in that information?

Now think about what happens when you combine green light with red and blue light—ever seen the amount of information you receive from a television picture? With just three different *flavours* of waveform, we can create complex interactions and images, so just imagine what we can do with the huge range of ambient energy fields we use when working with our subtle senses.

The biggest obstacle that most people face when starting to work with energy is how to deal with something that is intangible and infinite. In our physical existence, we are unable to comprehend

much about energy and how it works, except for the smallest fraction of information, so we tend to perceive it as we would a solid object.

We think that to travel from one place to another we have to move there—so surely, this is what energy must do? This is how we perceive energy as functioning. From the perspective of energy the story is very different because at the speed of light there is no space and time by which to judge movement.

The next issue when working with energy is that of separation. In physical terms we perceive things as being separate bodies, surrounded by air (liquid, vacuum, etc.). This separation is, however, an illusion in energetic terms because all energy is connected. There is nothing outside of that connection, so in energy terms there is only oneness.

We can intellectually understand this concept, but to actually put it into practice is much harder.

Next, we tend to have the habitual response of connecting to the facets of energy that are associated with the physicality around us. This means that rather than seeing energy as something that is always available to us, we tend to limit our *energetic sphere* to the room, location or physical space we are in.

This has remarkable consequences when we are sensing energy and what these sensory messages actually pertain to.

We must also take into consideration the idea of *perspective* and the further dimensions of energetic realms; for whenever we perceive energetic waveforms we are viewing them from our own, unique perspective and can only ever see a fraction of the many layers that exist as part of that waveform.

Energy works within infinite dimensions and we function in only three dimensions. You can say that we work in five dimensions if you include temporal and spatial dimensions, however some find it hard to conceptualise this.

The PsyQ consultant aims to work with something that they cannot comprehend or understand beyond a limited perspective. The experience of this perspective is very alien to us, especially when we first encounter it. Most people can only ever grasp snippets or snapshots of these experiences and do so in a way that is completely unique to them.

Add to this the various limits that are imposed by terminology/ language and cultural/social implications and we can see why the skills offered through PsyQ are seen as a gift!!

We shall be exploring ways to alter your perception of the world around you (and within you), to expand your viewpoint and gain a greater insight into the usually unseen realms that exist beyond our previous awareness.

At the end of this journey, your individual perspective will still only encompass an insignificant acquaintance to the infinite vastness of energetic realms, but even a minute expansion of perception will offer you immense rewards.

Know Thyself

Integral to building a healthy degree of PsyQ is the nurturing of an ability to recognise the vibrational information flows through your body. Recognising, translating and understanding this information is the very foundation of PsyQ. It is a step that many who are attempting to cultivate their abilities overlook or rush through, but it is absolutely essential.

By learning to recognise and interpret this information, you will begin to experience many new layers of perception (synaesthesia), be this visual, aural, tactile or olfactory (smell orientated).

Many people have a preference as to what experiences they want to have and desperately try to obtain a response via a particular sense. The issue here is that we all work differently. So, it is important to focus on what you can do, rather than what you cannot.

If you want to experience visuals, but can only feel sensations with your hands, focus on your hands, not on your eyes. This training of the brain to recognise what exactly you are sensing will eventually lead to evolving your other sensory experiences and you will begin to see, hear, feel and smell synaesthesia in full sensory spectra.

Focus on everything you sense and remember not to overlook anything—the more you glean from each exercise and practice session, the more confident you will be.

Our recognised five senses communicate with, and are translated by, our brains. However this process is not equal, as your brain will favour the information it gleans from some senses over others. The way your PsyQ decodes vibrational sensations will depend on the sense(s) your brain works with most and the type of synaesthesia you have.

Most people actually start to increase their PsyQ by sensing with their hands, because our hands (nerves) are actually very sensitive; on the whole, much more so than our other senses.

By offering your brain a clear energetic message and then recognising it consciously—*Yes I felt that*—you are telling your brain what to focus on. Once it knows where to look, the other senses will be adjusted to focus in that area also. This can happen at any time during your practice and, in some people, a particular sense will light up very quickly!

By learning to understand your body and the way your brain interacts with it, you will increase your PsyQ abilities very quickly. Taking time to acknowledge sensations that are out of the ordinary, a flash of light, strange tone in the ears or unusual twinge in your leg may appear to be a peculiar way of activating PsyQ, but it is a very good start!

An excellent way of working with your senses and developing brain-recognition is to practise on everyday forms of energy that are stronger than the subtle forms of energy we are aiming to interpret with PsyQ. Some good examples of these are electrical items, such as a television set or a light switch, mobile phones, light, sound and even people or plants!

Initially using your hands, feel the field emitted by a TV from greater and greater distances away from the set itself. Feel the energy of a light switch and then try to trace the cables that lead away from it, through the wall. Try sensing the EMF field of a mobile phone, especially when connected on a call.

Try to sense sounds with your hands by placing them in front of the speakers when you are playing music, then move further and further away from the speakers until you can just about recognise the sounds.

Do the same with a light bulb or if you have a light catcher/prism, try to feel refracted sunlight with your hands and even attempt to decipher the different colours of light. Working with people and other living things can be an excellent way to learn, as you endeavour to recognise fluctuations in their energetic fields.

Try sensing the energy fields around you in a different way. Rather than listening to music, try to see or feel it—what does light *sound* like? By altering the way we perceive strong electromagnetic fields (EMFs), we can learn to perceive the vibrations of energy that have greater subtlety.

Once you have practised with your hands, try to adapt your practice, using your other senses—so try to see sounds and hear light, etc. Of course this cannot be done by just looking at sound or listening out for light—if it could be, we would all do it consciously without the need for development! No, you are seeking to recognise your synaesthesia—your internal sensory interpretation, based on the vibrations you are sensing.

When starting to look at energy, try staring through the field, as if you are gazing at something in the distance and allowing the energy to appear in *soft focus*. This will work even better in half-light, so try practising in a dark room, by candlelight or with the curtains drawn.

When attempting to hear vibrations of energy, try emulating the reaction of your ears to a very harsh, high-pitched sound—imagine fingernails down a chalk board as best you can, then relax and direct the sensation towards the energy field. Do remember that when you are listening to light, close your eyes and make sure there is as little surrounding sound as possible.

The sounds of energy will be very slight, but it is important not to dismiss them, as your brain will simply learn to discount, rather than recognise the sounds of energy fields. As with all synaesthesia, in the beginning it is more fragile than usual sensory experiences. Eventually your experiences will be stronger than the usual sensations you are conversant with.

The Processes of PsyQ Development: Summary

Everything is created at a fundamental level from energy: energy that is both intangible and infinite. Energy can be experienced in an extensive array of *flavours*, depending on the frequency and amplitude, in addition to other factors, such as the perspective from which we perceive the energy. Some flavours of energy fall into the range of frequencies that we can sense with a high degree of PsyQ.

When we have the ability to sense these particular vibrations of energy, we can learn how to decipher information, which provides us with various degrees of sensory experience and knowledge regarding the specific facets of energy we encounter. The interpretations form the basic abilities of a PsyQ empowered person and can be enhanced to very powerful levels.

In order to develop these skills, there are several characteristics within us that need to be nurtured and improved. These include holistic self-healing, repatterning of the subconscious beliefs or statements that limit us, automatic entrainment of the body and mind that helps us to work with the PsyQ without the need to think about it, alteration of our perception and mastering the way we personally interact vibrationally.

There are also other factors that will help our development and these include the capacity to meditate, to focus, to be aware and to create.

You can picture your PsyQ development by seeing yourself at the centre of a sphere—a sphere of perception. Everything that you are consciously aware of forms the surface of this sphere, although there will be other layers or surfaces, depending on your degree of awareness, subconscious perceptions, etc. When your consciousness layer reaches the vibrational layers where your PsyQ is most effective, you will be able to leverage your PsyQ in remarkable ways.

A good appreciation of energy, in addition to knowing the way you *work*, will create an excellent foundation when it comes to expanding your sphere of perception.

Once we have achieved an insight into how our sensory skills work, we can then learn how we individually perceive energy. This is only half the story, however, for once we have learned the sensations of energy from our own perspective, we need to learn it from the viewpoint of itself (energy). This will enable us to see how energy functions in much greater detail and unlock a huge array of new abilities.

When it comes to practical exercises for the enhancement of PsyQ skills, it is regularity that counts, rather than the length of each practice. It is recommended that you practise between twenty minutes to one hour per day on this journey, however it is better to do five minutes per day than two hours once a month.

Testing the reaction of adventurers over many years has shown that those who practise on a daily basis, not only achieve better results, but also tend to obtain greater degrees of health, wellbeing and confidence.

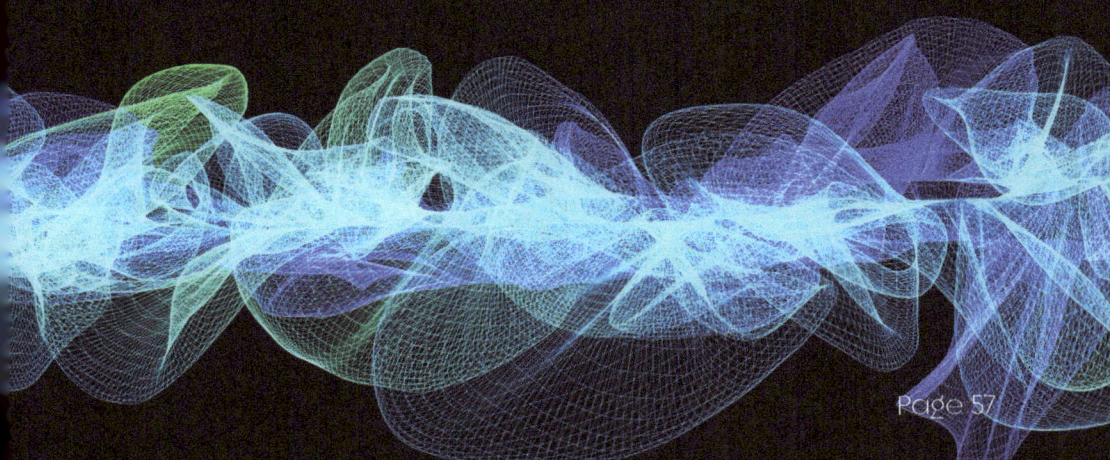

FOUNDATIONS

The Foundation Techniques for PsyQ Development

Raising your PsyQ is achieved in many different ways—the scope and approach to creating an increase in PsyQ is an exciting and varied adventure that results in an ever greater variety of skills. To begin with, however, we investigate a series of foundations that will give you a starting point—in many ways, your development is a gradual and multi-faceted process.

There are many different skills that you will encounter and these exist at increasing degrees of complexity and power. We shall begin with the basics and build upon these to create a toolkit of many hundreds of different techniques and methods.

These foundations will help you boost your PsyQ in the early days of study and propel you to the place where you begin to experience what an enhanced PsyQ feels like. As you expand into a vast range of techniques, tools and methods, you can always revisit this set of tools when you need to.

We start with some breathing techniques that will help with your relaxation, sensory and intuitive abilities. In these early days, getting some fundamental, physiological tools under your belt will really help.

Very few people know how to breathe in the most beneficial way and fewer actually breathe appropriately without thinking about it! Working with the mechanics of breath so that they become natural and subconscious methods will be essential to the future adventures we undertake on this journey and beyond.

The following routines will also help to improve your health and wellbeing, your vocal abilities and will make the practicalities of PsyQ techniques less challenging when you begin to work with the more advanced techniques.

Diaphragmatic breathing consists of a slow, deep, regular inhalation that creates a side-movement of the abdomen; you can check this by placing your hands in the concave of your abdomen, just below the ribcage.

Count up in seconds as you breathe, keeping the numbers regular and attempt to increase this number every few days. As you exhale, gradually relax your diaphragm, while pulling your lower abdominal muscles inwards (contracting the perineum when necessary). As you become proficient in this technique, your abdominal muscles will begin to move backwards and then upwards.

Pay close attention to these points, which expand when inhaling and contract when exhaling

No movement in shoulders

Pull low abdominal
muscles inwards
and up on inhale,
then release on exhale

We convert the messages from our subtle senses into intuitive information in the brain. The quality and accuracy of that information depends on how your brain is functioning at any given time and your brain state will have a great impact upon what you experience.

Your brain state can be categorised depending the frequency of the brainwaves you are producing. These different *rhythms* place us into four common *states*, which relate to the hertz measurement of your brain state vibrations. These are called *beta*, *alpha*, *theta* and *delta*.

- Beta 14-50Hz—Wide awake
- Alpha 8-14Hz—Very relaxed, heightened creativity
- Theta 4-7 Hz—Meditation or light sleep
- Delta 1/3-4Hz—Deep sleep or unconsciousness

When we are in a relaxing alpha or theta state, we can connect to our PsyQ much better than in the beta state. This is because in the alert and somewhat stressed beta state, our brain is just too busy to deal with this very subtle information.

By placing our brain into alpha state, we consciously access parts of our mind that we do not usually contact and therefore create a strong link between these and our conscious mind. This process could be equated to a light meditative state in which the subject is awake and yet very relaxed.

In addition to assisting us with subtle sensory and synaesthetic information, this magical state can help improve memory, intuitive responses and creative impulses as well as encouraging psychic awareness.

The technique we can use to click into alpha state is very simple, yet incredibly effective. It works on the premise that if you can get your brain to believe that it is in alpha state it will be in alpha state!

Clicking into Alpha state

Imagine eating a lemon, visualise biting the skin and tasting the zest, feel the bitter juice running across your tongue and before long you will start to salivate—your body thinks that you really are eating a lemon because it cannot tell the difference between the imagined and the actual.

Now, when we access a part of our brain, say to do some mental arithmetic or to recall a vague memory, we direct our eyes to the part of the brain we are accessing. This is known as eye-tracking and is an excellent way of noting what part of your brain you are accessing at any given moment. Do be aware that some people align with a usual tracking pattern, whilst a few have reverse pattern tracking, where their eyes track to a mirror image of the brain area.

When we are creating something, imagining a mental image or making up a story, we instinctively look up and to the right. The reason for this is to access alpha state, since this is the state that we are at our most creative and the portion of the brain that triggers alpha state is located in the front, right section of the brain.

If we direct our eyes to look up and slightly to the right for a length of time, we actually make our brain believe that we are in alpha state and we click into that rhythm automatically. To most people, this routine creates a sense of relaxation and serenity, yet does not affect their being alert or awake for any activity that is to follow.

THE TECHNIQUE:

Sit in a comfortable chair, where you will not be disturbed for a few minutes, and close your eyes. With your eyes remaining closed, look up and twenty degrees to the right, as if staring at a clock face and looking to one o'clock.

Hold this eye position as you count down from a hundred to one in your head—each number counted with a two-second gap left in-between.

When you finish this exercise you will be in alpha state!

If you find during the exercise that your eyes have drifted away from the position; just gently bring them back to twenty degrees. Additionally, if you lose track of your countdown, simply return to the last number you remember.

The trick with this technique is not to try and relax, but to focus on what you are doing; on holding your eyes at twenty degrees and counting down. This stops you from being distracted by random thoughts whilst your brain does the rest.

If you do this technique every day, you will train yourself to click into alpha state quicker and quicker, until you can start to decrease to seventy-five, fifty and so on.

Eventually you will simply click into alpha state whenever you need to without this exercise, however this does take time, so do not rush the process.

Autogenic training was created around 1932 by Johannes Shultz, who observed the physiological effects of warmth and heaviness in patients who were in a hypnotic state. He deduced that if you recreated these sensations in a particular manner, you could activate a meditative or hypnotic state. The practice was thus named *autogenics* or *self-created*.

Primarily used for stress management, autogenic training (AT), can have many physiological effects, such as regulating blood pressure, increasing concentration, relieving insomnia, assisting with weight loss and also as a meditation aid. We can also use AT to set up goals or aims, which can then underlie manifestation routines or even psychic development routines!

One of the big advantages about using AT as part of your daily routine is that it is simple to learn and does not require the ability to meditate. It is therefore very useful to those who find meditation or self-hypnosis difficult to master. The main disadvantage is that it is not an instant process, it is learned over a few weeks and requires 5-10 minutes of practice, three times a day.

AT works by using various *formulas*, which are repeated consistently in a particular way—so for example, you initially say,

"My right arm is heavy," several times. By repetitively instructing your arm to become heavy it will eventually do so, without conscious effort.

Translate this to your legs, chest, stomach; it is not long before you can instruct your metabolism to speed up, your blood pressure to reduce or your asthma attack to fade away! You can eventually add formulas, such as…

"I am aware of energy"

or

"Come forward, (your name)"

This command is an integral part of the trance work we shall be investigating later on our journey.

The key to AT is regularity—in order to work, it must be done daily, especially in the beginning. Working with your formulas just after waking and just before going to sleep, will make the process more effective, so even if you can only do these times every day the process will work.

Of course, try not to focus too hard when doing the routine, this is often counterproductive, as you are aiming for relaxation, but the focus you place on the exercises will hinder this. So just complete the routine in a very relaxed and matter-of-fact way, without trying too hard! Also, never do an AT routine whilst driving or operating machinery!

PREPARING FOR AUTOGENIC TRAINING

When conducting an AT exercise, it is always a good idea to sit or lie down in a relaxed and comfortable position, ensuring that you are in a place where you will not be disturbed or encounter sudden, distracting sounds, etc. Avoiding coffee and other stimulants will help and try to avoid a full stomach when practising.

Now before you start your AT practice, the first step is to learn the *cancelling process*, which is the formula that cancels all the effects of the training—you do not really want to go around with heavy arms for the entire day! The cancel formula is used whenever you are using the exercises.

To cancel, simply say: "Arms firm, breathe deeply, open eyes, come forward (your name)."

Then, in this order, clench your toes tightly and stretch your arms, take some deep breaths and finally open your eyes. It is important that you stretch your arms and breathe before opening your eyes.

The First Step of Autogenic Training: Inducing Heaviness

"My right arm is very heavy."

If you are left-handed, change this to "My left arm is very heavy," or if ambidextrous, choose which arm you would like to work with and stick with that same arm.

Repeat this formula in your mind, imagining it written or visualising somebody saying it to. Do not speak it out loud and if you find your mind wandering during the exercise, simply come back to the formula, without becoming frustrated with yourself. Should sudden ideas, thoughts, memories, etc. appear, it is essential that you do not attach to them, paying them very little or no attention.

Repeat the formula six times, followed by: "I am completely calm."

So, the first routine is as follows:

"My right arm is very heavy." x 6

"I am completely calm."

"My right arm is very heav.y" x 6

"I am completely calm."

… and so on, for 5-10 minutes.

Then use the cancel formula.

If at anytime you feel as if you are falling asleep during the routine, add the following formula and repeat several times: "I am staying awake and alert while training."

Complete this routine on twelve separate occasions and then go to the next step.

THE SECOND STEP OF AUTOGENIC TRAINING: INDUCING WARMTH

"My right arm is very warm."

As with the previous routine, swap to the left arm, if you are left-handed or choose an arm and stick with this same arm if you are ambidextrous.

In this routine, you repeat the first formula six times, followed by: "I am completely calm," then go on to the second formula six times and stay with this second formula for the rest of the routine.

So, the second routine is as follows:

"My right arm is very heavy." x 6

"I am completely calm."

"My right arm is very warm." x 6

"I am completely calm."

"My right arm is very warm." x 6

"I am completely calm."

… and so on, for 5-10 minutes.

Then use the cancel formula.

Contraindication: Do not say, "My right arm is very hot," as the language we use has a major impact on the exercise.

As with the first routine, complete this routine for twelve practice sessions, then go on to the next step.

THE THIRD STEP OF AUTOGENIC TRAINING: THE HEART PRACTICE

"My heart beats calmly and regularly."

Here you use the first formula six times, followed by "I am completely calm;" the second formula six times, followed again by "… completely calm;" and then you use the third formula for the rest of the routine.

Do not simply repeat all the formulas in a cycle—it is important that you only use the first and second formula once, before repeating the third several times.

The third routine is as follows:

"My right arm is very heavy." x 6

"I am completely calm."

"My right arm is very warm." x 6

"I am completely calm."

"My heart beats calmly and regularly." x 6

"I am completely calm."

"My heart beats calmly and regularly." x 6

"I am completely calm."

… and so on, for 5-10 minutes.

Then use the cancel formula.

Contraindication: Do not say, "My heart beats calmly and slowly."

As with other routines, complete this routine for twelve practice sessions, then go on to the next step.

THE FOURTH STEP OF AUTOGENIC TRAINING: THE BREATHING PRACTICE

"My breathing is calm and regular."

Now you use the first, second and third formulas in single sets of six repetitions, before working with the fourth formula for the rest of the duration of the exercise. When using this formula, try not to actively influence your breathing—simply repeat the formula in your mind, without taking your attention to your breathing.

The fourth routine is as follows:

"My right arm is very heavy." x 6

"I am completely calm."

"My right arm is very warm." x 6

"I am completely calm."

"My heart beats calmly and regularly." x 6

"I am completely calm."

"My breathing is calm and regular" x 6

"I am completely calm"

"My breathing is calm and regular." x 6

"I am completely calm."

… and so on, for 5-10 minutes.

Then use the cancel formula.

Work with this routine for twelve practice sessions then continue on to the next step.

THE FIFTH STEP OF AUTOGENIC TRAINING: THE ABDOMINAL PRACTICE

"My abdomen is flowing and warm."

Once again, we use the first, second, third and fourth formula and then fix our attention on the fifth and use this for the completion of the routine.

The fifth routine is as follows:

"My right arm is very heavy." x 6

"I am completely calm."

"My right arm is very warm." x 6

"I am completely calm."

"My heart beats calmly and regularly." x 6

"I am completely calm."

"My breathing is calm and regular." x 6

"I am completely calm."

"My abdomen is flowing and warm." x 6

"I am completely calm."

"My abdomen is flowing and warm." x 6

"I am completely calm."

… and so on, for 5-10 minutes.

Then use the cancel formula.

As with all the previous routines, continue using the penultimate step for twelve sessions before progressing to the final step.

THE SIXTH STEP IN AUTOGENIC TRAINING: THE HEAD PRACTICE

"My forehead is pleasantly cool."

In this final step, we repeat all the previous formulas in a single set of six repetitions, interspersed with an "I am completely calm," formula. Then you progress to the sixth formula and continue with this, until the end of your session. Remember to use the cancel formula at the end of the session.

The sixth routine is as follows:

"My right arm is very heavy." x 6

"I am completely calm."

"My right arm is very warm." x 6

"I am completely calm."

"My heart beats calmly and regularly." x 6

"I am completely calm."

"My breathing is calm and regular." x 6

"I am completely calm."

"My abdomen is flowing and warm." x 6

"I am completely calm."

"My forehead is pleasantly cool." x 6

"I am completely calm."

"My forehead is pleasantly cool." x 6

"I am completely calm."

… and so on, for 5-10 minutes.

Then use the cancel formula.

PSYCHIC DEVELOPMENT FORMULA

Once you have mastered the full routine, you can begin to modify your practice to encompass your PsyQ development. On this journey we shall look at individual formulas for you to integrate into your AT practice. Each time you are given a formula, encompass this formula into the routine below and repeat it between ten to thirty times.

"My right arm is very heavy." x 6

"I am completely calm."

"My right arm is very warm." x 6

"I am completely calm."

"My heart beats calmly and regularly." x 6

"I am completely calm."

"My breathing is calm and regular." x 6

"I am completely calm."

"My abdomen is flowing and warm." x 6

"I am completely calm."

"My forehead is pleasantly cool." x 6

"I am completely calm."

Personal Formula x 10-30

"I am completely calm."

"Arms firm, breathe deeply, open eyes."

An Anatomy of Autogenic Training

At each stage of the AT process, you are learning to use suggestion to create a physiological reaction in your body. This eventually works to have a major effect on the way you function physically, emotionally and psychologically.

From the outset, AT is working on your biological processes to create the desired results. The heaviness felt is caused by the increased blood flow around your body, as is the case with the warmth. As you progress to your heart, breathing and abdomen, you have profound effects on your heart rate, breathing and digestive system, before finally working on the brain itself with the final formula.

In time, you can actually reduce the formulas to simple, one-word statements: "Heavy, calm, warm, calm, heart, calm, breathing, calm, abdomen, calm, forehead, calm, personal formula, arms firm, breathe deeply, open eyes." However, do not try this until you are very experienced in your autogenic training and it comes as second nature to you.

The more you work through these processes over the weeks to come, the greater effect you will have with your PsyQ development.

The Perineum/Tongue Link

This routine, based on various energetic arts from the Far East, increases your ability to build the experience of energy. Excellent as a way of increasing your efficiency and potency when conducting any energy work, this method creates an increase in the amplitude around your body that effects you from your perineum, up the front of your body, over your head and down the spine, returning once again to the perineum.

The perineum, also known as the pelvic floor muscles, is located directly between the genitals/anus and can be contracted with a gentle pulling upwards, into the body.

Take a deep breath in, place your tongue to the roof of your mouth just behind the teeth and gently contract your pelvic floor muscles (perineum).

As you exhale, release the muscles and relax your tongue.

Energy Cultivation Technique

Sit quietly and relax in a place where you will not be disturbed for the duration of the exercise. If you want to, you can light some candles, use essential oils/incense and play some soft, tranquil music as these will calm the senses and help them to relax more. Place your feet firmly on the floor and close your eyes.

Focus on your breathing and take several deep breaths, directing the breath into your lower back and sides, allowing your stomach to rise with each in-breath and fall as you exhale. If you can, expand your chest to the sides as you breathe in—this will activate your lower lungs.

Place your hands on your stomach just below your belly button and leave them here for the duration of the exercise.

Now imagine that you are sitting inside a bubble of light. You can see this as a glow or feel it as a heat or vibration. Visualise this image as best you can and then take another breath in, sucking in this bubble of energy until it has been completely absorbed into your stomach—around the area where your hands are touching.

As you breathe out, blow away any tension, thoughts or stresses from the day and see the bubble filling with light again, collecting it from the air around you.

Now repeat this exercise and this time add the following steps to the breathing: as you breathe in, place your tongue to the roof of your mouth, just behind the teeth and at the same time gently pull up your perineum or pelvic floor muscles.

As you breathe out, lower your tongue and relax your perineum. Continue these steps throughout the entirety of the exercise and when you want to finish, simply come back into the room, open your eyes and take a moment to gather your senses.

Done every day, this simple technique will become second nature and it will greatly improve your energy sensitivity to the point where you can not only sense spirits, but also communicate with them.

Bubble Bounce

In conjunction with your energy cultivation technique, you can learn to sense energy with your hands. This is due to your hands being a very sensitive part of your anatomy and also because energy is very strong in the hands and tends to be focused there. By working initially with your hands, you will develop your other senses that will interpret the information collected by the perineural tissue in your hands and conducted to the brain for analysis.

The following technique will help you to sense vibrations and decipher key information from those vibrations, which include how the vibrations affect you, your understanding of the vibrations and so on.

THE TECHNIQUE:

Stand or sit in a quiet place where you will not be disturbed for the duration of the exercise. Close your eyes and place your hands out in front of you, ensuring that your palms are facing each other and shoulder-width apart. Try to keep your hands flat and parallel to each other while maintaining a good posture; shoulders open and relaxed, your spine straight and head up.

Start to take deep breaths; breathing into the base of your spine and with each in-breath, you feel your chest expand to the sides and your stomach rise. As you breathe out, your chest returns gently inwards and you allow your stomach to contract without forcing it. Your shoulders should not move at all when you breathe.

Now imagine as you breathe in that you are sucking in light, as a luminescence, sound, heat or vibration; the light collects in your hands and you are pulling in so much force that the walls, floor and ceiling of the room begin to bend inwards.

As you exhale, the light is projected from your hands with such power that the walls, ceiling and floor are pushed outwards so that they form a ball as opposed to a cube shape. Continue this for a few more breaths, projecting the energy from your hands until you feel heat, tingling, trembling or your hands actually start to move apart as the force pushes them away from each other.

At this point, start to bring your hands slowly together until you find an energy field or resistance and, when you get this, bounce your hands on it; this is rather like bouncing your hands on a balloon and feeling the resistance of the air inside except here there is no balloon and the resistance is often described as *magnetic*.

At this point become aware of the skin on your palms and the sensations you are feeling there. Try to experience this sensation as much as possible and attempt to bring that sensation up your arms, past your shoulders and into your head. The more you can do this, the better you will learn to sense vibrational fields.

As you cultivate your connection to your senses using PsyQ, you will find that you experience a range of effects that can at first seem strange or may create feelings of uneasiness. These experiences and your feelings towards them, are all very natural and are a wonderful sign that you are rapidly improving both your PsyQ and the skills that are powered by it.

As people go through the process of discovering their subtle senses, the effects they often report are varied and range from pleasant to *not so much*! The experiences are similar to those of calibration and can also include...

Erratic sleep patterns, feeling spacey, heat/cold, sweating or fever, feeling as if you are vibrating, palpitations, irregular heartbeat or chest pains, hypersensitivity to lights, sound, odours, touch, etc. You may develop numbness in arms and legs, skin rashes, vomiting and diarrhoea, tinnitus (beeps and sounds in the ear for no reason), headaches and pressure in the head, flu-like symptoms, aches and pains. You may find yourself becoming dizzy, clumsy and can even suffer from temporary memory loss.

You may also find that there are changes in eating/drinking habits, disappearing/blurred vision or objects fading in and out. These are all a temporary and very natural part of the healing and clearing process that will help you leverage your PsyQ much better. Of course, if you are concerned, please visit your therapeutic practitioner or a medical doctor.

You may shift between spiritual and logical patterns; go through phases of self-rebuke or of under-valuing yourself. You may feel special/unique intermingled with feeling abhorrent or even feel alienated from the everyday world—somehow different.

You may become more individual or experience increased creativity. You may experience less fear/more trust, periods of doubt, resentment and confusion or a desire for simplicity and clearing. You may feel a sense of

Discovering Your Sensory Self

urgency or needing to rush, fear of your own power, be unable to deal with the responsibility of your gifts and develop feelings of shame and frustration and other symptoms of emotional clearing.

You may find yourself overcoming addictions. You may encounter re-occurring issues over and over again. You may change your job, home, relationships etc. You may find that you attract like-minded friends, find you are able to say no more often when appropriate and find release easier. You may find that light bulbs flicker or blow out, electrical equipment malfunctions or breaks around you.

You will become more aware of your PsyQ experiences and may begin receiving dreams and visions of the future, which are often apocalyptic in nature. You may shy away from detrimental environments and your sensitivity to vibrations may become more pronounced. You can have mystical experiences, dreaming while awake and feel awake while dreaming. You can trust inner guidance more and meditations may become integral to your routine.

You may begin to instantly manifest and coincidences/synchronicities may become increasingly common. You can even experience extreme joy and effortless living, perfection and enlightenment.

These effects contain elements that are both pleasurable and painful, yet you will find that the most joyous effects become lasting additions to the way you feel and think, while the not-so-nice effects are just temporary and will pass very quickly.

The initial calibration of this Home Experience will help boost your sensitivity to PsyQ, along with many other features which offer a great foundation for your sensory enhancement practice.

There is another technique you can use to help increase your sensitivity, where you learn to sense vibrations of energy in a small, enclosed place such as a room of a house. You can adapt the technique to work with vibrations in any environment and it is very effective when working in nature or places with high levels of disruptive vibrational miasma such as offices.

By sensing energy in this way, you learn how to interpret your feelings into other types of sensory information such as seeing and hearing. Eventually you will recognise so many different vibrations of energy and become so adept at doing so that the less sensitive parts of your body will also sense it.

This evolves to such a degree that, in time, you will be able to decipher vibrational secrets in a holistic way (with every aspect of your being). When this happens, just by encountering energy of different vibrations, you will see, hear, taste and smell it as well as feeling it.

THE TECHNIQUE:

Practise this exercise in a place where you can be alone and without interruption for the duration of the routine. Standing in the corner of a room, centre yourself and focus on your breathing. Become more and more relaxed as you pull your breath down to your lower back and expand with each inhalation. The more centred on how you feel, the better results you will get.

When you are ready, place your hands out in front of you and start to project vibrational waves from them, taking a moment to feel the surface of your palms. Once you have done this start to move along the wall of the room, pushing the air in front of you. This is not just moving; it is trying to *hook in* to the resistance of the air, almost allowing it to push you backwards and having to resist it with a concerted effort.

As you do this, be very aware of all changes that you can feel in your hands and try to describe these as best you can. You may like to jot down words that describe the sensations and get into the practice of finding words that describe specific frequencies of energy.

If you come across a strong resistance in the energetic fields you encounter, *bounce* your hands along it to try and decipher the boundaries/ shapes of this resistance and see if you can work out what it may be—be aware of any images that come into your mind at this time.

Try doing this exercise around plug sockets and light switches as well as TV sets, VDUs, computers and other electrical equipment. Try living things such as plants/trees, animals and people—you can also try minerals and other *inanimate* objects.

Remember that as you learn to sense the world in different ways from those you are used to, you must not dismiss things because they **are** not what you were expecting. Very often we believe that we are going to *see* this or *hear* that and when these do not happen we think our senses are letting us down, whereas the inspirations, thoughts and flashes of insight, the colours, sounds and smells are all dismissed, as that is *not what it's supposed to be like*.

The sensations you are receiving are synaesthetic in nature, which means they are internal experiences of sensation, based on contrasting sensory feedback. Synaesthesia is a profound effect of increased PsyQ and a subject we shall explore in the Home Experience.

Projection/Reception Techniques

Next we turn our attention to vibrational projection and reception, with a look at some of the techniques you can use to affect vibrations of energy at a certain point or location. This will also improve how you can receive vibrational information using the same philosophies.

There are three different forms of vibrational projection, all of which rely on visualisation and intent, yet they differ greatly in results that can be achieved.

The first technique is *Contact Projection*, which consists of actual or very close contact to the focus object, location or person. Here we establish a link to the vibrational range of the focus by touching it or placing our hands a few inches away from it.

Next we come to *Distance Projections*, which work by interacting with the vibrations of a specific focus point from a distance; this distance could be the length of a room or the other side of the world and beyond. Examples of this technique can be seen in remote treatments or the power of prayer.

The result we seek to achieve when conducting this technique, is to experience a shift in perspective (vibrational shift) travelling outwards and towards the focus of the activity. We conduct distance projections purely by visualising the focus in our minds or directing intent at a proxy or substitute, such as a doll instead of a person or a box, instead of a house.

The final and most recent form of projection included here is *Direct Projection*, where we alter our own vibrational state to connect directly with the focus wherever and whenever they are. Once a connection has been created, we then change our energetic vibrations to where we want the focus to be. This produces a shifting in the vibrational state of the focus.

This method is the most energetic in viewpoint, hence the most effective.

Reception works in much the same way, except here, we perceive information or vibrations rather than projecting it outwards. Therefore, *Contact Reception* is the technique where you make contact with the source, either by placing it in your hands, placing your hands around the source or positioning your hands near the source. We then connect to it and sense the vibrations of the source, ready for the translation processes to take place.

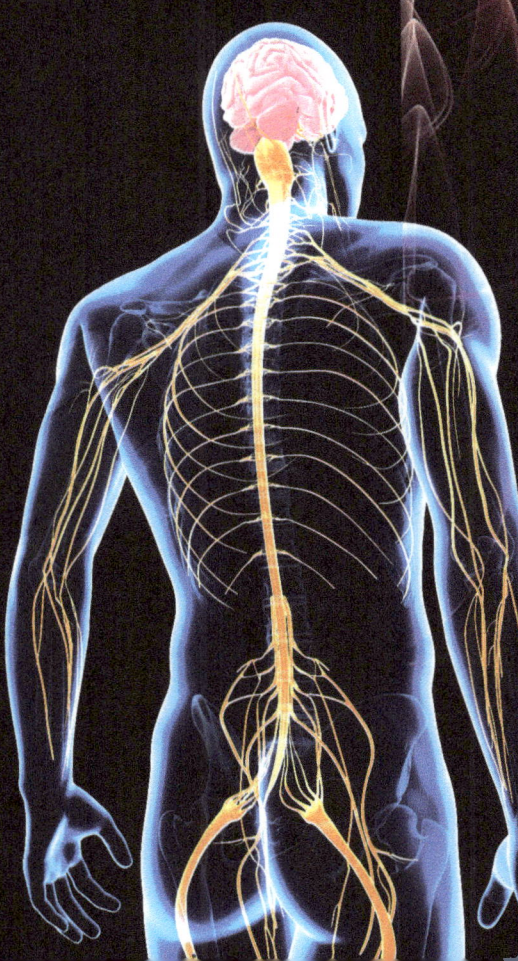

Next we have *Distance Reception*, which is where you sense the vibrations or information at a physical distance, as seen in remote viewing or astral travel. Here you visualise the vibrations travelling towards you from a source point (physical location), whether this is known or unknown.

Finally we have the *Direct Reception* technique, which is once again the most recent development in reception methods we cover here. In this method, we alter our energetic vibrations to match those of the source, thus connecting to it. Once we match this vibrational state, we can read the information from our body, instead of sensing at a physical distance (which is always more limiting in success and challenging to visualise).

Next, we encounter a highly valuable and popular technique that offers a basic yes/no system of answers to questions that you ask. It is a great means of meaning information about a vibrational field if you are finding the sensory experience confusing.

This tool works in the same way as dowsing rods or a pendulum, where the pendulum or rod moves in response to the environment or to questions asked by the practitioner. Here, no equipment is necessary, because your body is the main tool.

The Yes/No Technique or *Human Pendulum* as it is sometimes called, works by creating a backwards and forwards motion of the body in response to questions. These movements relate to either a *yes* or *no* response, depending on the individual person.

Traditionally, people have assumed the pushing/pulling sensations associated with this technique to be physical

Yes/No

interaction with some form of entity. We could also speculate that this is a dramatic synaesthesia reaction to the vibrations you are sensing, as clients being treated in holistic energy therapies also comment on the same sensations during treatment.

Simple to use, this technique requires you to stand upright, with your feet parallel and shoulder-width apart, your knees soft, shoulders relaxed and spine/neck/head straight, yet relaxed. Take a few deep breaths and relax before asking your question.

After the question is asked, or sometimes during the asking, you will be pulled forwards or backwards—this will give you the response you require and can be deciphered by your personal responses (i.e. you go forwards for *yes* and backwards for *no* or vice versa).

The orientation of the response may remain constant for you. It may change on each communication session or change randomly/on specific occasions. Therefore, it is advisable to calibrate the responses on each use, by asking for a *yes* and a *no*. You can also ask personal questions with true and false answers; "Is my name…?" or "Am I *x* years old?".

Yes/No

Activate/Deactivate the Arena

Your personal *Arena* is a powerful tool that will help you achieve sensory and communicative results. Practising the simple activation and closure methods will offer a good grounding for future reference. The Arena acts as a vibration *location*, within which you create a personal/neutral environment for vibrational and energy work.

To activate your personal Arena, locate eight points in the room to create a cube; this will be easy in a square room, but you may have to be creative in a triangular room, for example! Connect up the eight points to form a visualised cube and with this in your mind, activate the Arena by repeating the trigger three times (Arena, Arena, Arena). You can use the trigger barcode in the above picture to strengthen your connection, if you wish.

Stimulate the Arena vibrations at each of the eight points of the cube and then at all points inside the cube, including within your body. You may feel a shift in the ambience of the room as you do this or discover other effects, such as pulling and pushing, lifting up, pressure or tingling, etc. Whatever happens, it is exactly right for you and will change/evolve over time.

To deactivate the Arena, simply visualise yourself stepping out of the cube and into the room. Sometimes it helps to visualise a door in the cube or even a trapdoor that you can jump through!

Self-treatment is essential to increasing your PsyQ because underlying issues divert attention away from your PsyQ and towards the dis-ease, injury or trauma. The more integrity and depth you can achieve in your healing practices when working on yourself, the better and faster your subtle senses will start to interact with your brain!

When calibrating to the first PsyQ orientation, you will have learned a powerful perspective of energy that is very effective when it comes to self-treatment. This adaptive and versatile perspective can be used throughout our journey through the realms to assist your personal healing programme and develop your PsyQ skills.

There are many methods by which you can perform a self-treatment. The simplest of these is to place your hands on your chest or stomach each night when you go to bed, then shift to the treatment perspective of energy (Self-Treat x3) and gently drift off to sleep!

Variations on this theme can be done as often as you like and the more regularly you conduct the routine, the greater the benefits. It is a perfectly safe form of treatment and can create major changes and beneficial results on many levels.

For instance, begin by sitting comfortably in a place where you will not be disturbed for around twenty minutes or the duration of the treatment. The effects of the treatment can be enhanced with the use of music, incense and candles to produce a mood conducive to healing.

Once you are prepared, close your eyes, sit with your back straight and place your hands on your chest, stomach or lower abdomen—whichever is most comfortable for you.

Now simply say in your head, "I want to heal—to help me release dis-ease and old, unhelpful patterns of behaviour. I ask my higher-consciousness to guide this treatment for my highest benefit and most fulfilling purpose."

Then simply relax and allow the treatment to transpire for around 10-20 minutes, longer if you have the time. For the most

The Self-Healing Treatment

1—Temples
2—Crown
3—Occipital Ridge
4—Face
5—Neck and Throat
6—Shoulders
7—Chest
8—Solar Plexus
9—Sacral
10—Base of Spine
11—Knees
12—Feet

effective results, practise twenty minutes each day or for one hour, two or three times a week.

If you find that you do not have much time in your life to conduct treatments regularly, try running through the routine last thing at night when in bed and ready to sleep. Then, as the treatment starts, you can just drift off and experience your treatment whilst you sleep.

However, if you want to conduct a more elaborate self-treatment, the following routine will be most beneficial.

Sitting in a chair (1-12) or lying down (1-10), shift to a treatment perspective (Self-Treat x3) and place your hands on treatment position 1 (Temples). Hold this position for three minutes and then move to the next position, 2 (Crown) and so on.

Once you have completed each step, return to the temples for a further minute before completing the session. Then take a moment to come fully back into the room and have a drink of water before continuing with the day.

Your intuitive abilities are simply how you interpret the information you sense. The more practice you have at interpreting this information and the more descriptively you can do it; the more you will experience in future.

Intuitive description based upon what you sense, creates a reinforcing cycle that enhances your sensitivity. It is an important part of the process of nurturing your PsyQ, because we have so much going on in our head at any given time that we need to attach importance to the things we want to develop. The better and more elaborately you describe your sensory findings, the more you will pay attention to what you are receiving as you continue to work with PsyQ!

Very often, the method used to work with intuitive skills is based upon attempting to guess at things intuitively such as the shapes on cards or the colour of the next car to pass. While these are excellent ways of checking your progress they can really knock your confidence whilst you are learning, so are not advisable.

A really useful, confidence-building method for boosting your intuitive abilities is to work in situations where interpretation is at play. To start with, you work with purely vibrational foci, favouring those subjects that require interpretation rather than a single definite answer.

The reason for this is that if you are working on less than 100% accuracy whilst training (even most professionals are rarely 100% accurate), you can describe details of a historical place or person that can be verified and some of these details will be correct, some will be inaccurate and many will be unverifiable.

Getting some of the details right will boost your confidence— if you are guessing the colour of a car, you are either right or wrong; there are no margins here and incorrect answers do knock confidence.

Some people might suggest this takes your intuition to the level where you can just guess and get some right answers anyway through chance or luck. As you develop your skills, you will decrease your erroneous suggestions to zero and the accuracy of your information will increase to a very high level of truth with some unverifiable pieces here and there.

This comes from a mixture of experience, knowing how to interpret the sensory information you receive and confidence in yourself.

THE INTUITIVE ABILITY EXERCISE TECHNIQUE:

Stand in the centre of a room, in a quiet place where you will not be disturbed for the duration of the exercise. Centre yourself, close your eyes and bring your attention inwards. Turn your attention completely to your breathing, taking long, slow, deep breaths that cause your stomach to expand and chest to move outwards to the sides. Breathe this way until you start to feel relaxed and very calm—if you feel dizzy or light-headed, sit down for a while until you feel better.

Now, place your hands out in front of you, palms facing down and push downwards through the air until you reach a resistance. *Sit* your hands on this vibrational cushion and relax your arms into this resting place. If you want to, you can internally ask for help from some other benevolent source.

Many people do find additional help very useful at this point and who you ask for this help is entirely up to you. You might also decide that you prefer just to work under your own steam, in which case, ask to connect to *higher levels of consciousness*.

Now ask to be shown *the energetic patterns of the room* and wait for a response. This response should take the form of a slight *magnetic* pull in your hands which should direct one or both of your hands to the left/right. You may also find this sensation pulling you forward or back and do be prepared for this with your *soft* knees. If the pull takes you beyond the comfortable reach of your arms, you can walk slowly in the desired direction.

Search for changes in energetic vibration and continue to explore these changes until you find a vibration so *heavy* that you cannot push through it without using muscle effort. Bounce your hands along these heavy vibrations, until you have a good idea of the boundaries.

Then push your hands further into the vibrations of energy—if the force is too strong and pushes you back or resists completely, push the fingertips of your left hand into the barrier, creating a claw with your hand that *pierces* rather than pushes.

Once you have done this ask, in your mind, "What is this?"

Clear your mind as best you can. If you have trouble with this, try practising the alpha state exercise. Allow images, words, feelings, sounds and so on, to fill your mind. You mind find it helps at this point to clarify what you perceive by saying aloud your experiences.

Upon completing this, come fully back into the room, have a seat and take a moment to compose yourself and make any notes.

Chapter Summary

Do You Know?

To attain the required level of knowledge for this aspect of your PsyQ journey, you will need to be conversant on the following topics and areas:

A basic understanding of the following methods/terms:

- What we mean by the term PsyQ
- Orientations & Calibrations
- Vibrational Encoding
- Click Tracks
- The Foundation Techniques
- Arena Environments
- Energy Cultivation

Describe the differences, benefits and disadvantages between contact projection, distance projection and direct projection. Also describe the differences/benefits/disadvantages between the reception counterparts.

Understand the concept of what it means to increase your PsyQ from the perspective of this Home Experience and what we are attempting to achieve, in terms of expansion of perception and removal of limitations.

Be fully conversant with basic terminology of energy, including the following terms: frequency, wavelength, quanta, hertz, amplitude, modulation, waveform. Understand the effects of increasing/decreasing amplitude and frequency. Verbalise the importance of perspective in energy work, covering both individual-viewpoint-based and when considering the difference between human and energy perspectives.

To recognise why self-healing, repatterning of subconscious attachments, automatic training, altered perception and energy mastership are each important to PsyQ development.

- To conduct a full self-treatment
- To carry out the Yes/No Technique
- To activate an Arena
- To conduct a simple AT routine
- Correct diaphragmatic-breathing technique

Chapter Homework & Exercises

ONE: BREATHING EXERCISES

One of the essential exercises in PsyQ development is to breathe correctly. If you think about your breathing in relation to your mood—if you are anxious, stressed or undergoing physical exertion, your breathing becomes laboured, fast and erratic. When you are relaxed, your breathing slows, becoming deeper and more expansive. If you consciously alter your breathing patterns, your body and mind will also become calm and still, hence much more receptive to PsyQ sensory information.

Here you learned the basics of breathing that involve a sideways expansion of the chest, activation of the lower lungs and the muscle support of exhalation. Use this technique twice, every day, preferably first thing in the morning before your AT routine, and last thing at night after your AT routine. Each time, try to increase the count on the outward breath, starting from seven seconds and increasing to eight, nine, etc., on the next session. Keep the count the same throughout a single session.

TWO: AT ROUTINE

Conduct the AT Routine, listed in the additional notes. Start with step one for twelve separate sessions and then progress to step two for twelve sessions and so on.

THREE: SENSORY PRACTICE

At every convenient opportunity, attempt to sense some form of energy field. The list below will offer some suggestions. Use your hands to complete the sensing and jot down what you experience; journal your experiences in the realms.

Try the following, plus any other fields you find interesting (remember to ensure your safety when working with electrical equipment and do not work with exposed wiring, etc.):

- Light switches
- Cables in the walls
- A TV Set (electrical field, static and sound)
- A VDU (computer monitor)
- A houseplant or tree
- An animal
- A friend or relative
- Running water
- Music from a hi-fi
- Your hands
- Sunlight refracted through a prism (sun-catcher)

FOUR: YOUR LINGUISTIC APPROACH

Get into the routine of monitoring the things you say in everyday speech. In particular, focus upon the words you use in reference to yourself, your PsyQ and energy. Working with the list of non-appropriate words in Appendix B, try to adapt your linguistic usage to create a more expansive approach in the words you choose.

FIVE: SELF-TREATMENT

Take twenty minutes or so, every three to four days and give yourself a relaxing, soothing self-treatment, using the routine listed in the additional notes. Better still, do the treatment routine when sitting watching telly or in bed at night— whenever you get the chance to sit/lay down and relax.

SIX: ARENA

Work with triggering your personal Arena and journal any results you get from this practice, including how the sensations/occurrences evolve over time.

HOLISTIC HEALING AND TRAUMA CLEARING USING YOUR PSYQ

The initial priority of anybody wishing to increase their PsyQ is to remove any obstacles that are diluting or diminishing your abilities. These include trauma or injuries from the past, current dis-eases, emotional or mental issues and so on. This requires an exploration of holistic therapeutic treatments, often referred to as *healing*.

Working with low-frequency energy to create a suitable environment for healing is a very rewarding part of PsyQ work. Treatments include self-healing, but also treatments for other people— this mix of personal and professional treatments not only benefits the clients you treat, but will also improve your own PsyQ abilities.

Regardless of how you apply your PsyQ abilities in the future, a good foundation of physical, emotional and psychological wellbeing will improve your successes in profound ways. Many people who proactively work with PsyQ comment upon how their skills are diminished at times of ill health or when not feeling on top form. Thus regular treatments are vital to maintain a high PsyQ

With the sphere of perception philosophy you expand to a specific frequency range of vibrations in order to increase your PsyQ. To do this, you need to heal yourself so that past trauma and dis-ease do not hinder the expansion process.

Let us build upon this foundation with the creation of an *energetic rescue kit* which can be combined with a trance-like state and a group of additional techniques to create a powerful modality of energy therapy.

Using this therapy to heal yourself and others, you will hone, refine and boost your PsyQ to new levels of expansion because, not only are you healing yourself at every stage, you are also learning how to use your intuitive skills to decipher how best to help people.

People who use energy therapies on a regular basis often find their PsyQ improves without them even knowing it existed. As you can imagine, this often leaves the therapist feeling somewhat bewildered especially when they enter trance or start seeing things around them during treatments.

Yet, imagine what heights these same abilities could reach if you combine them with a focused PsyQ practice, strategic exercises and the potent tools we have yet to discover in this Home Experience! Building upon innate abilities as a by-product of therapy is powerful, however when you guide your growth and development with volition the results are deeply profound and life-changing.

As we investigate the nature of healing with energy-based treatments and how this combines with your other PsyQ practices, we shall also examine the wider aspects of holistic therapy—understanding the person, rather than the symptoms they exhibit. This revolutionises the way you comprehend health and wellbeing.

As with all therapies, there are many factors outside the actual learning of the therapy that require your attention; such as the processes of consultation and the legal requirements for therapists to acknowledge. It is important to include this knowledge as part of your study if you are planning to work professionally with your therapy.

In an allopathic medicine a physician will treat an illness or injury as and when it occurs. If you have a headache, it is treated with painkillers. If your blood pressure goes up, this is treated with beta blockers. If you have a bacterial infection, you will be prescribed antibiotics. Western doctors examine *the bit that is going wrong* or what physiological problem is causing the illness and then attempt to fix the symptoms.

A holistic approach has been used for thousands of years and was around long before orthodox medicine came to be. Holistic therapy starts with a very simply premise: treat the person, not the symptoms of disease. This has many interpretations that sadly often focus upon a fraction of the philosophy or get the wrong end of the proverbial stick.

Have you ever accidentally cut your finger with a knife?

Initially you are aware of the cut, probably because of the pain signals that are transmitted through the nervous system. You then administer some first aid and eventually forget about the cut, it heals and all is well.

This is so seemingly mundane that is it often missed—the cut heals without any conscious interaction from you—this is amazing!

The healing process is completely automated: your body heals itself using the components of a physiological system in your body known as the *living matrix*. This demonstrates how your body actually wants to heal its injuries and hurts. If something is not as it should be or the survival of the body is at risk, it will do everything it can to fix the issue.

The usual view surrounding dis-ease or injury is that we experience pain (or other issues), because of the dis-ease/injury. Yes, if the dis-ease was not there, we may not have a high temperature; if the injury had not occurred, we may not experience the pain, but you should remember that it is not the flu virus that creates the temperature. It is not the injury that causes the pain, it your body's reaction to the injury: a subtle, yet significant difference.

Your body raises its own temperature to kill off the invading virus—you want to rid yourself of the virus and heal any damage. Hence, a completely automated system swings into action and your body's reaction to the virus becomes apparent. Your muscles ache, as you need to preserve your strength in order to fight the invasion, you may crave certain foods or substances that your body needs and you might get a temperature to combat the virus.

As we know, a temperature in extreme cases can kill a person. Why would the body fight so hard to fend off an invading virus that it actually destroys itself? Are there some things, such a danger to us, we would rather die fighting than let them conquer us?

The body is programmed to survive—it is built into us at a genetic level. Our genes want to survive and reproduce, so it is paramount that we survive injury and illness without lasting detriment. In situations where the dis-ease or injury is too powerful to be healed, the body will literally die trying to survive.

One of the first challenges we face here is that when we get the flu, we do not want to rest—we have work to do! We don't want that pain—it hurts! So we take decongestants and pop painkillers that basically tell our body to shut up! We treat the things that our body is doing to prevent the virus from spreading, instead of treating the underlying issue: why the virus is there in the first place!

This leads us to the holistic approach of treatment—as opposed to focusing on the dis-ease itself, we focus on why the person has the dis-ease. Hence we treat the person as a whole, including why they need to be unwell as well as what it is about their particular issue that is good for them.

Yes, the logic does seem strange at first, but let us understand how having the flu can be good for a person as a whole…

Working in the highly-pressurised environments of the IT industry, where the product or service was fundamental to success (and everything was sacrificed to that end), I discovered just how important holistic wellbeing was. With a skill set that was very specialised, I became much sought-after in the industry, commanding a huge salary and industry-wide respect; I had the life that many people dream of attaining.

I was not happy.

I wanted to believe in the product or service I was creating: if I was going to work towards the success of that product or service, I needed it to make me feel good: I wanted to help others, to learn and to be spiritual. Eventually, having witnessed several young people, who were much younger than I, taking drugs in the office toilets, simply to get through the day, I knew something needed to change.

Still I resisted and eventually there was only one option left for me— get sick. I decided on a subconscious level to develop flu-like symptoms.

For the first few weeks I tried to get into work—I took painkillers and dragged myself in on the Underground each day, only to be on the point of collapse by the time I started work. It was so important to me that the job got done that I actively attempted to work against the healing processes of my body.

Eventually, however, I gave up and took to bed where I stayed for three weeks, thinking, reading and meditating.

When I returned to my job, I lasted four days before I resigned and set myself up teaching Usui Reiki. Having the flu had given me three weeks of rest, healing and the time I needed to make life-changing decisions. As I went through that transformation process I realised that being ill had offered me something that I would not have had without it: a new life.

Many, many people around the world transform themselves because of illness. All dis-ease and injury creates change within us, although these changes are usually so minute that we do not notice them. This illustrates how a physical illness may not have a physical foundation, instead, stemming from a need for change on another level.

For me, the flu was needed to give me the time to think, rest and change my life through emotional, cerebral and spiritual transformation. As I had not made changes in the normal routine of my daily life, something was going very wrong with me as a whole—so my body took it upon itself to heal the problem.

In an orthodox sense, my body came into contact with (and contracted) a virus. In holistic terms, the stress and unhappiness caused by my job meant I was not only susceptible to a virus, but flu was exactly what I needed to heal the issues that were stopping me from attaining overall wellbeing. I used the disease of my body as a way of clearing dis-ease from my life.

This is the essence of the holistic approach: when a person is not functioning in a healthy way on one level, it will manifest as dis-ease or injury on another level (usually physical) to address the issue.

Examples of this are seen in vibrational medicine, when a person's ancestral line contains gonorrhoea and the person themselves has a tendency towards asthma because of this link. In vReiki practices, we use kuki to treat brain states, thus easing physical dis-ease and in metaphysical practices when a problematic left knee pertains to issues with a person's mother.

When a person's mind, emotions, body and spirit are all nurtured and functioning well, they are holistically healthy. The holistic approach views someone as a whole person rather than focusing on the symptoms they manifest. The holistic therapy treats that person in their entirety and thus perceives physical symptoms as a sign that the body is healing, so the holistic mindset understands that in order to heal; we often need to be dis-eased.

Modalities of holistic therapy, such as spiritual healing, energy therapies and vibrational medicine have been around for thousands of years and played a major part in our evolution. Reportedly used by the ancient Egyptians, Aztecs, Mayans and even further back, low-frequency energy or *spiritual force*, has been harnessed as a way of achieving health, wellbeing and enlightenment for many people throughout history.

In recent years an emergence of the therapy *Usui Reiki* has spawned a massive interest in energy therapies and other forms of spiritual healing. This new wave of popularity has brought with it a huge amount of interest from the scientific community and a greater understanding of how low-frequency energy works in both a healing and psychic environment.

In its simplest form, spiritual healing is merely a gentle touch and manipulation of low-frequency vibrations, whilst some modalities of energy therapy use powerful techniques and methodology to offer a massive range of treatment types.

To help you clear past trauma and heal holistically, initially for yourself and then for other people, we shall be using a mixture of PsyQ methods and vibro-energetic therapy. This differs from spiritual healing in a traditional sense as the method we will be working with has a foundation in contrasting philosophies to those traditionally associated with the religious background of spiritual healing.

This is so you can provide the best therapy for as many people as possible, rather than only treating those who believe in spiritual healing (or a specific spiritual belief system). The foundation principles behind a holistic therapy, how they adapt to a person's own beliefs and the openness a person demonstrates towards a therapy are all factors in how successful a treatment will be.

The Physiology of Vibro-Energetic Healing

Human anatomy contains a multitude of different systems and complex networks, which perform diverse tasks and regulate specific aspects of the physiological functions involved in our bodies. A select few of these systems create a living matrix that is at the core of treating people with any form of vibro-energetic medicine.

The living matrix consists of the perineural, perivascular, periosteum and perimysium systems, along with the digestive system and the skin.

The nervous system is a complex array of cells known as *neurons*. This *neural network* runs from the brain, down the spinal cord, to all the extremities of the body. It is through this system that sensory information passes from one point to another as electrical impulses.

For example, when wish to move your right index finger, you brain sends an electrical message to the muscles in your finger, via the neural network and thus creates a *point to point* communication. Once this has occurred, a message is sent back to the brain, declaring that the movement has taken place.

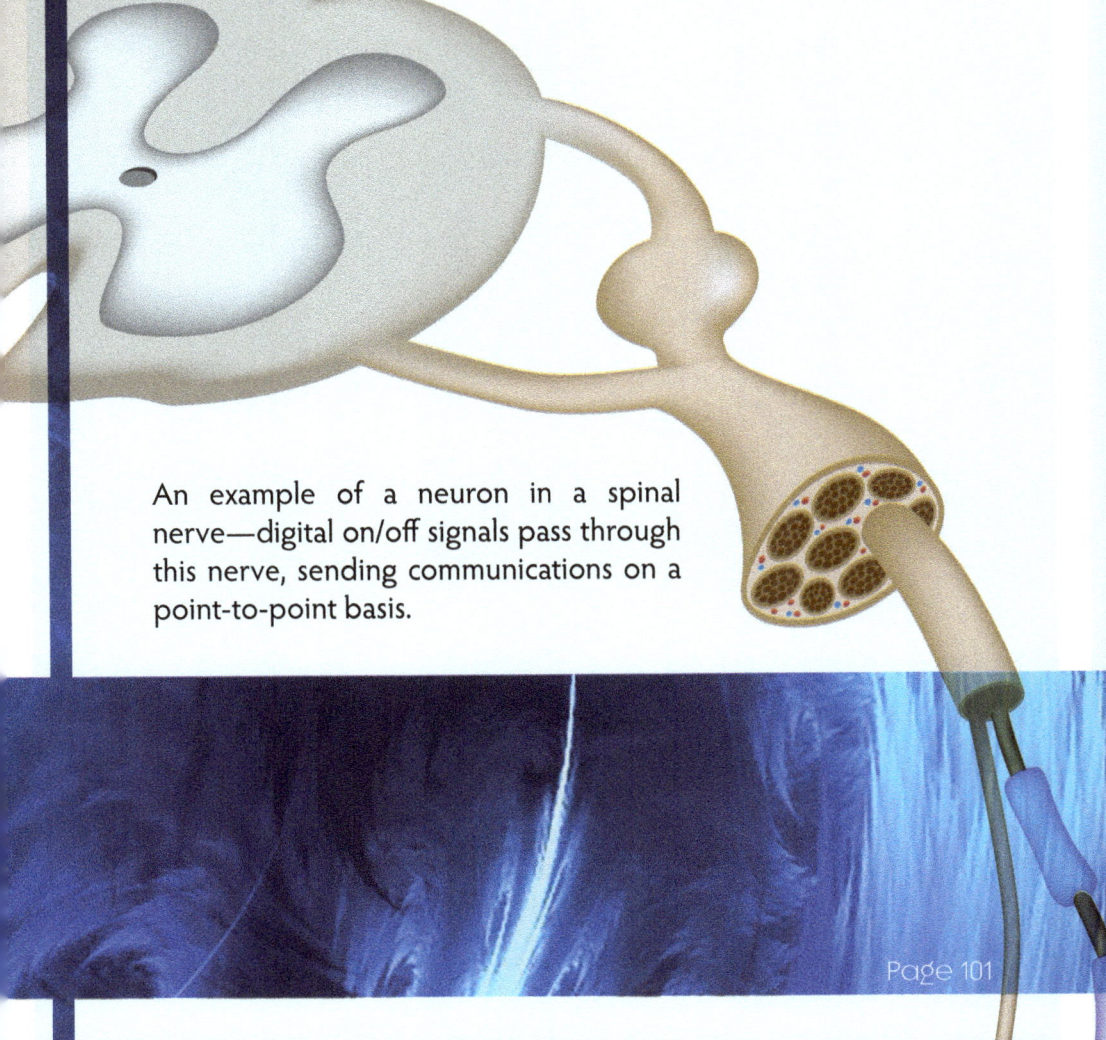

An example of a neuron in a spinal nerve—digital on/off signals pass through this nerve, sending communications on a point-to-point basis.

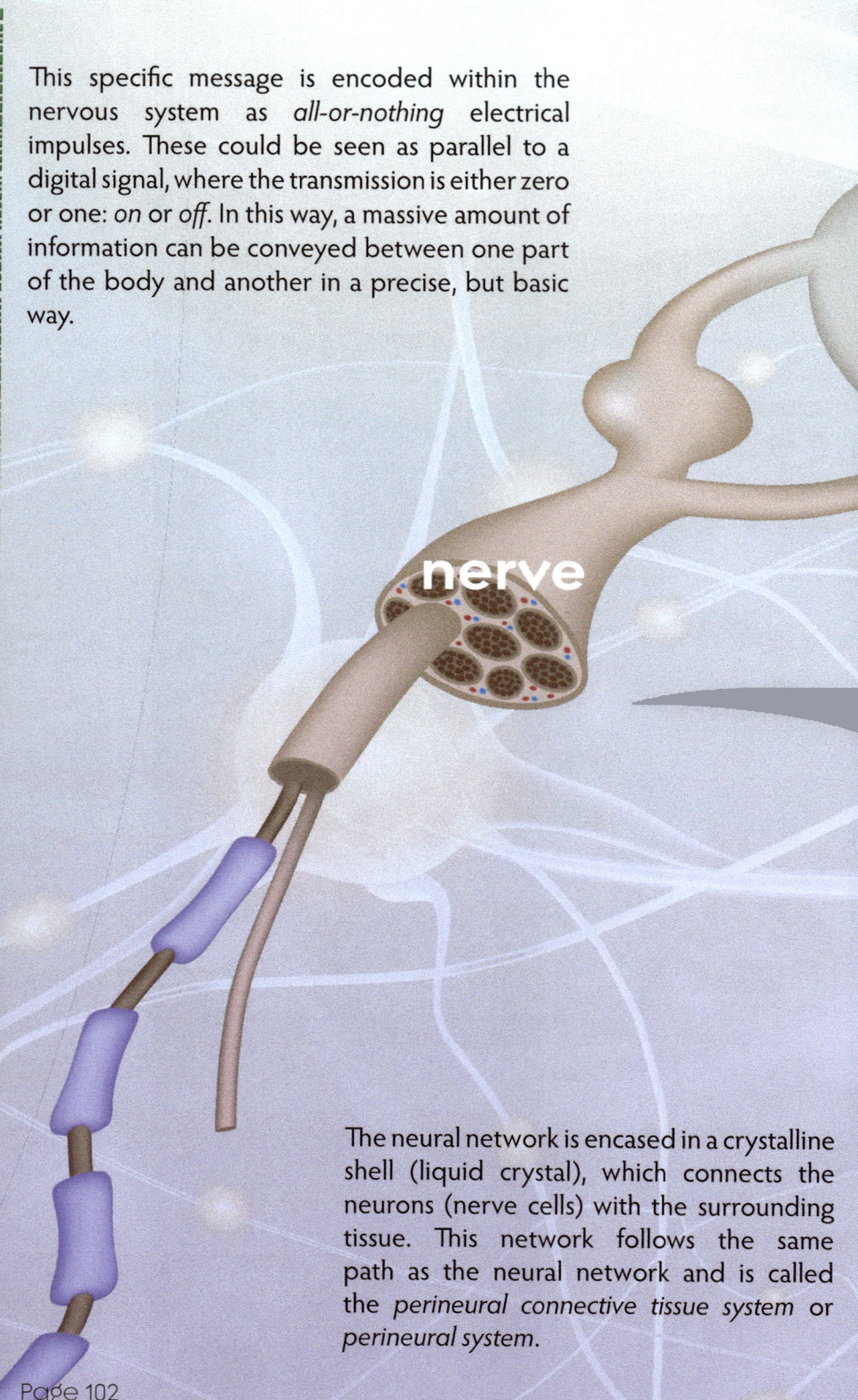

This specific message is encoded within the nervous system as *all-or-nothing* electrical impulses. These could be seen as parallel to a digital signal, where the transmission is either zero or one: *on* or *off*. In this way, a massive amount of information can be conveyed between one part of the body and another in a precise, but basic way.

nerve

The neural network is encased in a crystalline shell (liquid crystal), which connects the neurons (nerve cells) with the surrounding tissue. This network follows the same path as the neural network and is called the *perineural connective tissue system* or *perineural system*.

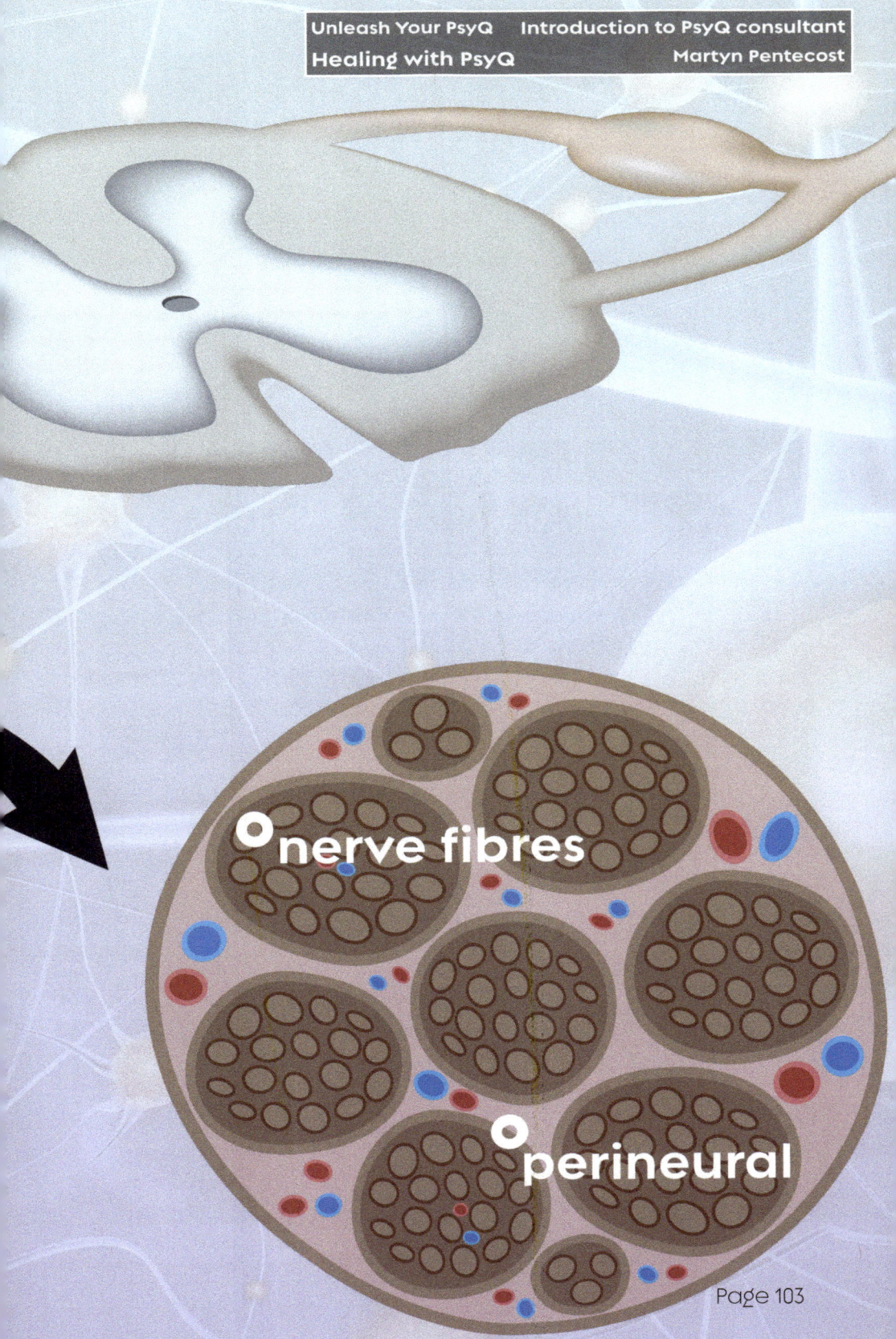

nerve fibres

perineural

The perineural system acts as the main constituent in supervising the body's natural healing activities. By coordinating with the brain the perineural organises the deployment of healing agents such as fibroblasts and white blood cells.

The perineural cells make up around half the cells in the brain, hence forming a massive amount of brain mass, yet the *messages*, communicated through the perineural system, take the structure of waveforms. These hold more detail than the neural impulses, but do not have the same volume, so often feature less extensively in overall brain activity.

The energetic waves that ripple through the perineural system create a global network, which communicates information throughout the entire body, rather than from one point to another, as in the neural network.

The general implications of this mean that when a person is injured, for instance, the perineural system will initiate and coordinate the repair and healing of that injury on a bodywide scale.

Research suggests that the perineural system is not under the control of the neural network, conversely, it actually governs the neurons and regulates the response of the entire neural network.

In scientific exploration of the effects when manipulating the perineural system, it has been

documented that this important system presides over the following aspects of physiological response:

- Activities such as navigation
- Psychological behaviour
- Reaction time
- Biological rhythms
- Anaesthesia and hypnotic state
- Control of growth and regeneration
- Injury repair

In considering these and the many other functions of the perineural system, various phenomena have been documented, such as those witnessed in the results of a high PsyQ.

This dual nature of the nervous system also translates to other systems in the body, such as the circulatory system. Every artery, vein and capillary is enveloped in connective tissue, known collectively as the perivascular system.

The electrical currents formed by the flow of blood through the circulatory system in turn create magnetic fields that permeate the entire body, thus forming an excellent communication system bodywide.

Add to this the periosteum system (surrounding the skeletal system) and the perimysium system (encasing each muscle) and we see these crystalline connective tissues are extensive through all the major systems of the body. Their vibrational and magnetic waves permeate every network, the surrounding tissues and beyond the physicality of the body.

Now whilst the vibrations conducted through the various peri-systems communicate information (in vibrational form) about the health of the body and any necessary maintenance work that needs to be coordinated, the peri-systems also conduct vibrations from outside the body.

These might be the emissions of a mobile phone or television screen, but they can also be more subtle, such as the state of emotional health of another person, the deeply hidden vibrations of their karmic/ancestral trauma or even experiences that exist beyond our understanding of the physical world.

Our peri-systems are excellent physiological receivers (and transmitters) for waves of vibrational energy. By learning to *sense* beyond the very loud noise of the neurons, blood vessels, etc., we can *tune into* these subtle energy fields and decipher a plethora of information. Learning to recognise peri-systems' communication, influence them and translate them into usable information is essential to developing your PsyQ.

Blood Vessels

Muscles

=

Living Matrix

Bones

Nerves

Skin & Digestive Tract

As a complex, interconnected system, your living matrix is designed to coordinate bodywide healing completely naturally and without conscious intervention. When working with a holistic approach to healing, all we need do is support the processes of the living matrix and we boost the body's ability to heal itself. By stimulating the perineural and other peri-systems, you not only reduce pain, but you are also compelling the body's own healing agents into motion.

As a whole, the living matrix not only affects your emotional (chemical) state of being via reactions in the cells and opiate receptors of your body, but also repatterns the hydrogen bonding of water and neurochemicals that are an integral part of your physiology and function.

Therefore, working with the living matrix affects the mind (nervous system), emotions (chemical system), miasmatic patterns (hydrogen bonding) and body (cellular results).

The living matrix communicates information bodywide for the purposes of self-repair and we can use this system of transmission to sense other forms of vibrational information. The next stage of the process occurs when vibrational communication creates a chemical chain reaction. This enables our body to share data at cellular and genetic levels.

The average cell works like a factory, producing various chemicals on demand, it is these chemicals that we use in our biological functions and have even been hypothesised as being fundamental to the way we feel emotionally.

The external face of each cell consists of a plasma membrane, which can be viewed as the *walls* of our factory. The membrane is covered in long, strand-like molecules, called *opiate receptors*, which penetrate the cell interior and travel deep into the cell.

At the centre of the cell is the nucleus, which contains our genetic information in the form of DNA and between the

Chemical Emotions

nucleus and the membrane is the cytoplasm, a water-based fluid that contains various manufacturing components, such as the ribosomes and the Golgi.

When the DNA in the nucleus is requested to do so, it unravels and creates a copy of itself known as messenger RNA or mRNA. This duplicate of the DNA then leaves the nucleus and is interpreted by the ribosomes and transforms DNA into a protein. This is created using amino acids. The Golgi then concentrates the proteins ready to be exported from the cell.

This production process creates chemicals (proteins) that are then released into the body for the creation of specific chemical reactions, depending on the particular type of protein. These reactions can take the form of a physical process necessary to life or can create further communications from cell to cell.

These trigger a production process in other cells that may even be at a completely different place in the body. The variety of different chemicals a single cell can produce is huge and scientists are still attempting to identify and understand many of these. Even the most basic single-celled organism has the capacity to produce seven hundred different chemicals!

Our physical bodies are saturated with a cocktail of chemicals that not only act as a method of communication, but also intrinsically affect the way our body works and functions each day. This foundation leads us to the conclusion that if chemicals effect our body and how it functions, they will therefore influence the way we feel and our overall health too.

These chemicals exist in a finely balanced synthesis and any one chemical may have an effect on many other different types of chemical in the body. Hence, this chemical matrix is directly linked to our physical health, however, by looking deeper, we can also see that the chemicals in our body also create what we have come to call our *emotional self*.

Some of the specific chemicals are called *neurochemicals*; an array of substances that fall into three main categories. The first of these are *neurotransmitters*, next there are *steroids* and finally, *neuropeptides*. To understand these fascinating chemicals and the part they play in our emotional experience, we must first look at another group of molecules, known as opiate receptors.

Opiate receptors are a range of long molecules that sit on the surface of every cell in our body. Each receptor penetrates the membrane of the cell and passes deep into the cytoplasm, thus forming a long strand of chemical elements that communicates external information to the host cell.

There are many different types of receptors, which basically sit on the cell vibrating, shimmying and generally dancing about, waiting for a corresponding neurochemical to pass by in the surrounding fluid.

Groups of neurochemicals, known collectively as *ligands*, can be viewed as chemical *key* equivalents to the opiate receptor's *lock*. When an appropriate ligand arrives at the site of a receptor, the two will fit together and cause a reaction that is passed down into the host cell. This causes the cell to do something—create another cell, produce a further chemical reaction or even for the cell to terminate itself.

This chemical communication therefore translates into a physical reaction once the receptor and ligand meet.

The first member of the ligand group, neurotransmitters, such as serotonin and dopamine, are usually created in the brain with the intent of carrying communications between the synapses in the brain;

Ligand

Cell Membrane

these are the gaps between one nerve and the next.

Steroids, made from cholesterol, are produced in specific areas of the body, for example, the ovaries or the adrenal glands. These control many anatomical processes, from development through puberty, to the way we react when we encounter a dangerous situation.

Then we come to the *peptides*, an intriguing element of the receptor-ligand relationship, as peptides are created in the ribosomes of our cells from the information of our DNA/mRNA. This means our entire body has the ability to create peptides and whilst many peptides are only produced in certain areas of the body, others such as enkephalins, can be created in every cell.

Peptides have, perhaps the most profound effect on us, as they are responsible for deciding when we are born and when we die, as well as having a major influence in how we feel every day that happens in-between.

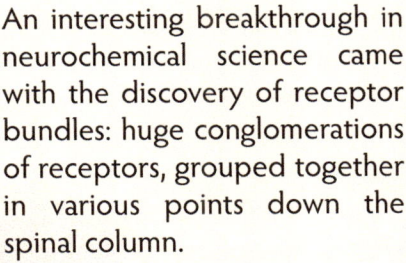

An interesting breakthrough in neurochemical science came with the discovery of receptor bundles: huge conglomerations of receptors, grouped together in various points down the spinal column.

These bundles act as massive sensors for the chemical emotions in our system at any one time. Whilst a particular steroid or neuropeptide may saturate our bloodstream, we may only be receptive to that particular chemical at certain points of the body—receptor bundles.

When we consider these areas, we appreciate that our bodies are chemical powerhouses at specific locations. The sites of opiate receptor bundles display fascinating similarities with two other systems. The first being anatomical: the endocrine system. The second is energetic: the chakra system.

As the endocrine centres and the receptor bundles both contain high levels of neurochemicals, we can say that these areas of the body are fundamental to the overall working of the body. These sites are also highly energetic and contain massive vibrational epicentres.

These not only overwhelm the living matrix with vibrational information, but also have important effects on our healing, wellbeing and PsyQ levels.

The popular view of the emotional self is often thought, especially by scientists, to be created by specific parts of the brain, collectively known as the *limbic system*. Electrical stimulation of areas of the limbic will produce a range of emotions in the subject: anger, joy, grief and so on. It has therefore been commonly assumed that the limbic system formed what was termed the *seat of emotions*.

When studies were carried out to locate twenty-two specific types of peptide; associated with various feelings—a staggering 95% of these were located in the limbic system. This demonstrated that whilst stimulation of the limbic system will create an emotional response, it is actually the production and reception of chemicals in the brain that is the main source of these emotions.

So it is hypothesised that rather than being a classical neurological seat of emotions, it is the chemicals in our bodies that determine the way we feel. This was a major breakthrough in many ways.

We can now see that emotions are communicated from cell to cell, as each receives ligands created in other areas and starts to produce peptides of its own to communicate the message to other cells. This can also make a connection between our emotions and our physical health, thus understanding why certain positive emotions can lead to better quality of life and holistic health.

Since its origination, neuroscience has discovered many more types of peptide and the associated receptors for each, becoming one of the most valuable areas of science. Embracing everything from PsyQ development and spiritual practices, to emotional health, psychology and even an understanding of how the AIDS virus works.

Hydrogen Bonding

All matter is created from basic building blocks known as atoms; these atoms come in different flavours, such as oxygen, copper, helium and aluminium. These *elements* can attach themselves together into larger formations called *molecules*, through a process where the atoms are bonded together.

The bonds that hold the atoms in molecules are created from a minute force and for the most part are called *covalent bonds*. There is, however, an exception to this and it is found in the bonds between elements that form molecules with the element hydrogen. When hydrogen links with other atoms it creates a *hydrogen bond*.

Hydrogen bonds are believed to store vibrations in the force that creates them. When a bond forms between a hydrogen atom and another atom of any flavour, it

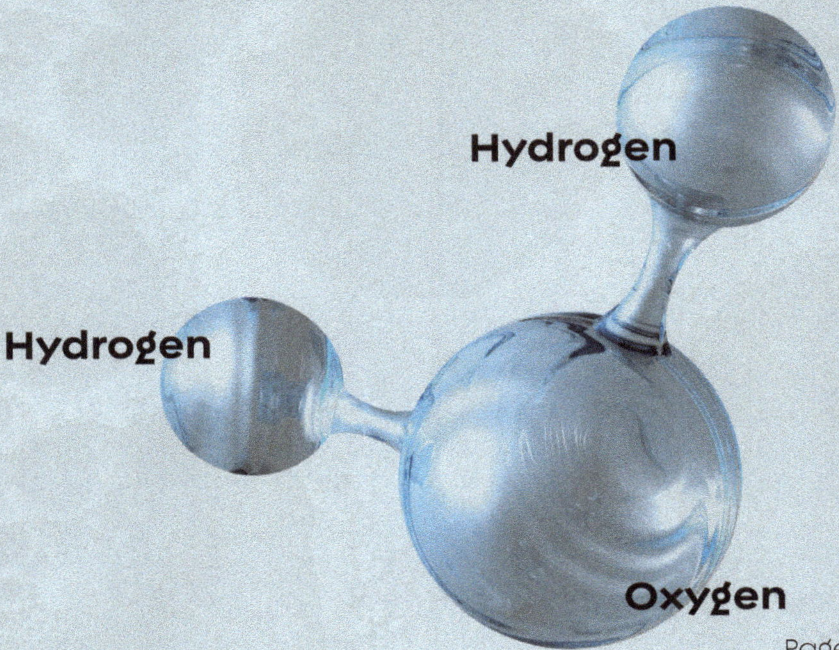

Hydrogen

Hydrogen

Oxygen

holds a set pattern, until it is changed by some other vibration that is stronger or repetitive. One of the most abundant forms of hydrogen bonds can be found in H2O or as it more commonly known, water.

Our bodies are made up of around 70% water molecules and the cellular tissue of the human body contains a huge amount of water. So, each cell in our body is a little encyclopaedia of vibrations: vibrations created from our environment, from our habitual, learned responses, from dis-eases and trauma and even passed on from our parents, grandparents, etc.

In addition to water, other molecules that have a high incidence of hydrogen bonding are the hydrocarbons. Hydrocarbons are long, complex molecules that have many atoms consisting purely of hydrogen and carbon. These long molecules can combine with oxygen and nitrogen to create a massive range of organic compounds that are even more complex in structure and essential to life. Sugars, lipids, amino acids, neurotransmitters and even DNA are created from these molecules.

This is one means by which vibrational memories contained within hydrogen bonds can be passed via the DNA from generation to generation.

At a molecular bonding level, vibrational information may be stored completely undetected, yet influences our bodies in profound ways. Memories of acute physical illness, extreme emotional trauma, psychological issues and even intense experiences could be contained at this integral level.

Vibrations in the molecules of the food we eat and the water we drink may also repattern our molecular hydrogen bonds. What is important to remember, however, is that these changes all take place on a vibration/energetic level. Physically the molecules remain the same, meaning that changes are undetectable even with modern equipment.

The specific form of energy therapy we use with PsyQ development is known as a vibro-energetic therapy, which is an evolved version of Lemuria Therapy. I personally originated Lemuria, launching the modality in 2003 and subsequently incorporating its methodology into aspects of Celtic Reiki, PsyQ and The Viridian Method… three of the modalities which now form One Therapy.

Here, the modality is titled vibro-energetics to distinguish it from the variants contained in other aspects of One Therapy.

Vibro-energetics does not rely on vibrations alone to achieve results: the perspective we *act from* is just as important. Unlike vibrational medicine, such as homoeopathy or Dr. Bach's remedies, the vibrations are replicated from the practitioner's perspective rather than actual vibrations from the source item. So what we see here is a therapy that is perspective driven—it is conducted from the practitioner's own perspective.

We have three different factors to our vibro-energetic therapy: *perspective, vibration* and *action*. By adjusting these three factors, we can achieve a wide range of different results when treating others and ourselves.

Once you have mastered these three aspects of treatment, you can adapt the therapy to create an energetic rescue kit. This can be adjusted to various healing themes; from healing the human body, to treating environments and beyond… depending on your sphere of perception and which layer of this you are working from. (Please read Appendix A to discover the elements of an energetic rescue kit.)

Another important aspect of vibro-energetic treatment is the Energy Alignment Process or EAP.

The *energy alignment process* is a concept used in some energy therapies and is conventionally known as a *healing crisis*. The EAP is a transitional period that can trigger various physical, emotional and psychological effects as the client adjusts to a new perspective. These effects usually only last a few days (if at all) and never manifest for longer than a twenty-one-day period.

During this three-week phase, a client may experience cold or flu-like symptoms such as muscle pain, headaches, blocked sinuses, nasal congestion, etc. They may also have emotional ups and downs

The Vibro-Energetics of PsyQ

and psycho-cerebral effects such as mild dyslexia, muddled speech, unhelpful or unwanted thoughts, even mild depression or anxiety attacks. A client may experience visual effects such as lights, flickering, strobes, etc., and also aural effects. These could include voices, tapping and so on.

At the end of each treatment, it is advisable to mention the EAP to your client and advise them to drink plenty of water during the time of an EAP. It is important that this is emphasised on the initial consultation with a client. Remember that, at any time after treating somebody else, you may also have an EAP as well.

There has been much (heated) debate as to whether the EAP is actually a symptom of the treatment or a psychosomatic reaction due to its possibility being suggested. Many practitioners thus chose not to mention the EAP. In vibro-energetics this is not good practice as hundreds of treatment case-studies by vibro-energetic and Lemuria practitioners clearly support a need for reassurance and rational explanation.

All dis-ease is actually an expression of the body healing itself so, whether or not the EAP is caused by a treatment or by suggestion, its very appearance is a very good sign that a person is getting better and is clearing on some level of their being.

Conducting a Treatment for Yourself and Others

Before conducting any treatments on yourself or others, please ensure you have calibrated to the VE therapy orientation, using the audio companion in the realms.

The *basic seated treatment* can be adapted for use on yourself and others. For you, simply sit in a comfortable chair and work through the steps on yourself. When treating professionally, your client sits in the chair and you, the practitioner, stand behind them. The chair should have a straight back and be at a height sufficient for you to stand upright without hunching over and place your hands on your client's shoulders.

This treatment will last around thirty minutes and consists of a simple series of hand positions. With your hands being held in each position for approximately six minutes. Each hand position is completed with fingers closed, palms flat and with each of your hands touching the client (or yourself) or held an inch or so away from their body depending on you and your client's preference.

Initially, begin with a *head connection*. This is where you place your hands on the temples and then take a moment to connect to yourself and your client. You will often feel this as a subtle shift in sensation. Once the connection has been made, trigger your chosen *essence* and work through the hand positions. These are:

Temples, occipital region (back of head), crown, face, throat, shoulders.

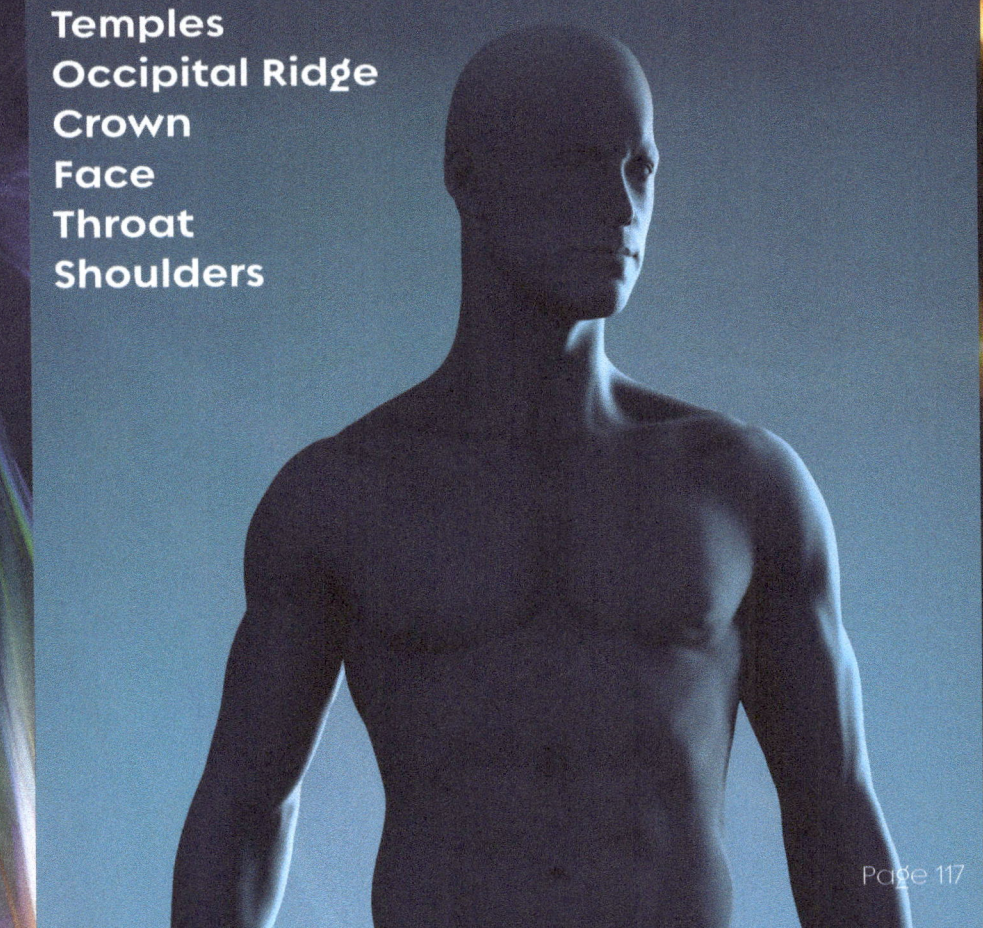

Temples
Occipital Ridge
Crown
Face
Throat
Shoulders

At the end of the treatment disconnect from your client, bring them back into the room and offer them a glass of water. Ensure that they are fully aware and coherent before asking them to stand up.

A variation on this, is where you choose three essences and hold each essence over two hand positions or two essences held over three hand positions. A treatment of this length of time should contain no more than three essences. You can also shape the essences but remember to limit your shapes to one per essence.

The second treatment we can use professionally is with your client lying down on a treatment couch, bed or sturdy table (obviously a treatment couch is preferable and a necessity for professional practice). In this routine, there are no hand positions as all treatment is done intuitively.

Once your client has lain on the couch, make sure they feel comfortable, have good back support and are at a suitable temperature, not too hot or too cold. For this treatment you should use between one and four different essences and shapes.

Begin, as before, by making a head connection and, after the shift of experience, position yourself at the side of your client. Activate your first essence and shape before placing your hands over your client's chest/abdominal region, palms facing towards your client.

Find a sensation, rather like a magnetic *bounce* and allow your hands to rest on this. Clear your mind and allow your hands to move gently around, pulled by the

magnetism. This is not a voluntary motion but a magnetic one that is totally without conscious interaction.

Continue with this motion for the duration of the treatment (forty-five minutes to one hour) changing essences and shapes as and when required.

The Essences

The implementation of essences and shapes from our energetic rescue kit can create highly adaptable forms of treatment. You can discover an in-depth exploration of the tools in Appendix A, however here is a summary for your reference.

- Sandalwood—comforting, soothing, releasing, general healing

- Salt—purifying, cleansing, suppression, unable to express emotions, anger

- Rose—softens the pain of unrequited love, love lost or grief

- Jet (Jet Mineral)—grief, sorrow, trauma of death, loss, depression

- Vacuum—loneliness, separate, feels disconnected or misunderstood

- Yellow (Yellow Light)—darkness, lonely, depressing, stagnant, still, lethargic

- Silver—confused or hectic energy, religious dogma, ME, hyperactivity

- Oak –weakness, drained, lack of strength, back pain, smoking, addiction

- Iron—boundaries, disconnection, clearing of residuals and unwanted vibrations

- Rowan—assertion, strength, urinary/fluid, kidneys, poor diet/malnutrition

- Plutonium—darkness, panic, fear, dread, repatterning

- 18Hz Essence is not used in treatment

The Shapes

- The Beam—simple connection
- The Pulse—penetrating
- The Spiral—increased potency
- The Echo—repatterning
- The Triangle—problem-solving
- The Arena/Sphere—sanctuary/nurturing
- The Hypercube—4D healing

Each essence and shape is triggered from the perspective of a healing treatment and is activated through the calibration to the VE orientation that accompanies this region of our PsyQ adventure.

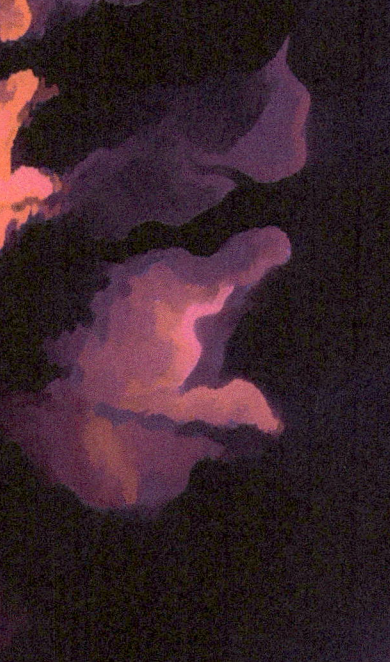

This version of *psychic surgery* is a technique to remove deep-rooted trauma that might be blocking a person's progress. These *vibrational memories* are often seen as the root cause of dis-ease and, while present within a person's sphere of perception, can cause great anguish and instability. The pain of the past often remains until it is actively repatterned thus provoking the host to react in a contractive way towards the vibrations.

Psy surgery is a very effective way of dealing with traumatic aspects of a person's perception and can be beneficial in the alleviation of physical, emotional or health issues. In many ways, the routine involved in a psy surgery session is as much an intellectual or visualised practice, as it is an energetic one.

By talking through the visualised aspects of the treatment, you are helping the client to focus on their most painful issues without connecting to them. As they do this, you will also become aware of the vibrations and can repattern them using the physically based extraction movements, which are an excellent way of focusing on and shifting the traumas in question.

The Technique

Firstly, your client must want the issue resolved and therefore this technique relies on their total co-operation. It is imperative that the practitioner spends some time with the client assessing the situation.

Once the client is seated comfortably, ask them to describe the condition to be healed. Have the client visualise the condition and ask them where in the body they believe the condition to be residing. This would not necessarily be in the obvious position. Migraines caused by stress may have their root in the chest area, for example. The client knows best where they feel the condition to be.

Next ask the client to identify a shape, colour, texture, weight, density, motion temperature and even the smell of the condition to be removed. It is important that the client does not connect to the issue at hand, but imagines fictitious parameters for the traumatic object.

Thus identified, both the practitioner (using their intuition) and the client (using sensory information) can assess any shift in sensation.

Psy Surgery

The client then needs to actively meditate on letting go of the blockage, creating a willingness to assimilate any knowledge or lesson gained from the experience.

1. Rub your hands together vigorously.

2. Activate the plutonium essence and echo shape.

3. Acting assertively and with definite motion, pull your fingers visualising that they extend to approximately nine inches (imagine you are taking off a pair of gloves and pulling each finger in turn). Take an in-breath during this process and repeat it twice.

4. Stand or sit in a balanced and upright position. Focus on the area your client described as being the root of the trauma. When ready, assert the essence/shape and push the visualised fingers into the area; it does not matter if the physical fingers make contact or not.

5. Visualise the extended fingers gripping the shape and withdraw them with a steady intake of breath.

6. Shake your hands as if flicking water from them.

7. Repeat this process for three to five minutes.

8. During this time, ask your client to concentrate on the area concerned and report any changes in sensation. The shape may have decreased, moved or even disappeared altogether. If the shape remains in any form, repeat until the client reports that the object has disappeared.

9. Ask your client to report any image or communication he or she feels, irrespective of how relevant it seems on an intellectual basis. You too must trust and say the first thing felt or received.

10. After finishing the surgery, place your hands over the treated area and switch to rose essence and spiral shape.

11. Continue with a seated or horizontal treatment.

To attain the required level of knowledge for this module of the course, you will need to be conversant on the following topics and areas:

- The holistic approach to treatment
- Understand the principles of vibro-energetic treatment
- Understand the energetic physiology
- Know all essences and shapes used in treatment
- Have a good knowledge of treatment types

Living Matrix—can you detail the various components of the living matrix and describe the difference between the workings of the neural & perineural systems, including communication method, function and physical structure?

Describe the different brain states in terms of name, frequency and general effect.

You should have absolute grasp of all legal requirements governing treatment, practitionership and other areas of therapy (Appendix C).

Good awareness of the consultation process, including all forms, paperwork and peripherals required. Appreciation for the dynamics, intent and required outcome of a consultation and a high standard of client care (Appendix C).

Be aware of contraindications and issues surrounding EAPs.

ONE: CONSULTATIONS AND TREATMENTS

Conduct as many consultations and treatments as you are able on family, friends or other adventurers in the realms—these can be face-to-face or remote in nature. Focus on any questions that arise, challenges you face or feedback that comes out of the treatment.

You should attempt to practise at least one of the following treatment methods: seated, horizontal and psy surgery. Remember to prescribe the appropriate essences and shapes, according to the consultation with your client.

TWO: APPENDICES

Work through the Appendices A to C and integrate the consultation, administration and legal elements, etc., into your understanding of vibro-energetic practice.

THREE: FOUNDATION SKILLS

Continue your work with the various foundation skills and techniques, identify the areas where you need to practise and implement the appropriate tools. Attempt to tie in each tool and technique with the appropriate foundation as listed in this chapter.

FOUR: JOURNAL YOUR EXPERIENCES AND SHARE WITH THE COMMUNITY

Chapter Exercises

Personal Readings and ESP: An Introduction

The ability to read and decipher the personal physiological vibrations of another is one of the most fundamental techniques available to us, both when developing our skills and for professional practice. The body is an immense array of vibrations, some of which can be detected scientifically, most, however, cannot.

For training purposes we have available, a smooth transition from reading strong vibrational patterns, akin to those of an electricity cable or light bulb, to ELF vibrations that are predominantly undetectable by modern scientific equipment.

This transition denotes a way of fine-tuning our PsyQ experience to recognise subtle vibrations; it also gives us a wealth of information to translate. It is in this translation that you can discover a foundation from which to work, for the physically created vibrations of energy are subjective and this means that interpretation is much more appropriate than hard fact.

Traditionally, the way to boost extrasensory perception (ESP) was to use Zener cards or similar tools to guess the future outcome of a specific process; this could be the subsequent card to be taken from the Zener deck or the colour of the next car to pass you on the street, etc.

The problem with these methods is that they tend to be cold, clinical gauges of measurement, rather than the interpretive, perspective-orientated ways of energy. Therefore, instead of encouraging a student towards an intuitive and creative translation of vibrations, they offer a test which tends to blocks sensory information, especially when the student is fearful of being tested.

Zener cards give the impression that there is a definitive response when choosing the exact symbol on the subsequent card. In other words, the next card in the deck is predetermined and unchangeable; therefore it is a matter of the PsyQ consultant *guessing* correctly.

This is a passive method of prediction—we walk a fixed line towards our fate and so prophetic information simply tells us what that line will be. An active method takes the approach

that we have infinite possibilities ahead of us and we simply choose which possible outcome we want.

In the case of Zener cards, it is possible that the next card in the deck could be any of the available symbols, if you decide it will be a particular symbol and then connect to that future, the outcome will be a correct prediction. This attitude to prediction is rarely taken, but it has a very high success rate and can greatly improve ESP, when the foundation mechanisms are in place.

If a PsyQ consultant is being tested with Zener cards and one of the core beliefs is that they *always fail*, it is invariably the case that they will guess the wrong symbol. Not because they do not have a high PsyQ, but due to their choice needing to connect to the future where their fundamental, core beliefs are proved right. Until we have removed our limiting beliefs, Zener testing and similar methodologies will give an inaccurate measure of ESP abilities.

Tradition tends towards a rudimentary development of the PsyQ experience then almost immediate testing, which works against the primary nurturing process, thus undoing all the benefits accomplished by the initial learning.

This not only pleases sceptical scientists, but also fortifies the bastions of the established *gift* philosophy used by many traditional psychic mediums. Of course, some forms of testing are encouraging to the student, yet these work on the basis of interpretation, such as that involved in personal readings.

The physiological processes of the body create vibrational fields of energy that extend way beyond the physical form, not only in physical space, but also in energetic state. These fields range from the very strong, to ELFs, and thus offer an excellent training ground in which to hone your skills.

Each vibration in this field presents us with a piece of information, advising us of a person's mood, state of health, memories, traumas, feelings and so on. When we start to sense this vibrational information and translate it, we are likely to work with words, images or feeling that resonate with the person you are focusing upon.

By working together, you can help enhance a person's ability to reach to the truth, rather than simply presenting them with a cold hard fact. This simple act helps the learning processes in personal readings, ESP and just about every other area of PsyQ development. Mastery of the personal reading will be one of the most beneficial elements for your study on this Home Experience.

In Western culture we use words to communicate our current state of being and even though only a small fraction of this communication is conducted via those words, we have become almost completely focused on them. This is at the expense of other forms of communication, such as body language and vibrational information. In our society, when we have an issue, we are inclined to talk about it with our friends, who will hopefully listen, advise, support and nurture.

On my travels, I have met with many other intelligences, whose cultures differ from our own. One particular series of encounters was with an intelligence who lives in a culture that uses energetic communication only (she does not have a verbal name, so we shall call her *Zener*, for ease of use). She has immense difficulty understanding our culture and social interactions!

In Zener's society, when somebody has an issue, everybody knows about it instantaneously and usually senses it before it has even occurred fully. When you perceive vibrations, you connect into those vibrations. Hence, one being's vibrations are everybody's vibrations: one person's pain is everybody's pain. So if an individual in Zener's world becomes dis-eased or feels contractive emotionally, everybody else feels it. The pain of one becomes an issue for all, so everybody endeavours to help the one, by healing the issue within themselves. Consequently, there is very little pain in Zener's world, no deceit and no secrets.

This may seem a nice idea, but far from relevant in our situation. Yet, if we examine the living matrix within our own anatomy, we understand that our physical/ chemical body does not use words to communicate from place to place, system to system—it uses vibrations (and chemicals triggered by vibrations). Just as Zener's people know when something is wrong for one/wrong for all, so does my body, your body, all our bodies.

Everything your body has ever experienced or has knowledge of will be contained in its vibrations and this is communicated to others. Each and every living thing uses this vibrational communication; we just tend not to do it consciously.

The more you increase your PsyQ, the greater your sensory and conscious experience will be of this oneness within us all.

By grasping the processes and dynamics of the human body, emotions and mind, we not only understand ourselves to increasingly deeper levels, but we also recognise those dynamics in others and between others. We gain an insight into the choices that are made and the consequences arising from those choices.

With an appreciation of the complex dynamics of life, we can pre-empt what is to come and change it. What is more, we begin to surpass the physical realms, understanding what is occurring beyond our usual conscious experience.

One of the most important factors when developing ESP for personal readings and other practices is that of perspective. Each and every person has a unique perspective, which is based on individual experience; including attributes such as cultural background, genetics, social community and so on.

Our individual perspective causes each person to perceive things differently from every other person in the world. We may have similarities and our perspective might be close to that of other specific people, but ultimately, nobody has a perspective exactly like any other.

We do however have baseline perspectives that we can work with. These are facets of energy that we all have a parallel awareness of. For instance, white light is a facet of energy that the majority of people have had experience of and can therefore recognise.

Regardless of where our perspective lies, we know the vibrations that create white light and despite *how we interpret* white light as a conscious experience, we *know* it integrally at a sensory level.

However, if you were blindfolded and placed into a room where various facets of energy were being projected at random, would you be able to distinguish white light from blue light, using your hands or sense of smell?

The chances are that, without training, you would be unable to do so because whilst your senses would be aware of the vibrations of white light, your conscious mind is only used to working with those vibrations via your eyes. However, if you go through the process of associating the vibrations of white light that you sense with your eyes, to the same vibrations sensed by your hands, you have a baseline with which to work.

Eventually, whenever you sense white light exclusively with your hands, you will actually begin to see white light with your eyes. This is synaesthesia—the way we decipher data from the subconscious to conscious thought by mapping sensory experience: we basically perceive images/sights/sounds that best represent what we are sensing.

If the vibrations of white light are most familiar to you via the seeing of white light, this is how your brain will translate the information—why invent a new image for white light when you see it every day and recognise it for what it is?

This is all very well, but what use is this to us?

We can actually sense a far greater range of vibrations with our hands than we can with our eyes, so if you connect to a subtle vibration that is outside the spectrum of visible light, you cannot usually see it. Yet, if your sight and touch are working from a baseline, you will actually see what your hands are sensing.

We can add extra dimensions to this when we add other people to the mix. As we all have an individual and unique perspective of the world around us, we can only ever perceive from our own perspective.

So if we attempt to read the vibrations that are perceived by another, we will only ever see our perception of their perception. So if you attempt to read their interpretation of white light via your baseline, without a point of reference to compare the baseline to, you may not sense white light, but something different.

We overcome this challenge by creating hand-to-eye associations with three common baselines. Once you can translate these baselines, you can judge the differences between your baselines and those of the person you are reading (your client). Three baselines will be sufficient to read and compensate for differences in three dimensions, all that we usually require for the basic reading.

Your baseline vibrations should be connected to things that you can have with you during every reading session that you do. This ensures that you can monitor your client's reaction/perspective to each of the three baselines. The easiest three baselines to work with are red, blue and green light, as these are usually available in any reading environment, as they are the comprising elements of white light!

Red

Green

Your Perspective

Your Client's Perspective

Blue

Learning to read red/green/blue light with your hands means that you can compensate for perspective in every situation where there is light. Even if we are in a situation where our eyes cannot perceive light, such as a dark room, there is still enough light for our hands to sense (think about the night vision mode of a video camera).

So, if we do require the use of our ESP/personal reading skills during an event that is held in the dark, even the minutest amount of RGB light will enable us to work with our baselines.

What is amazing about this method is that the people with you do not need to be aware of the light or the processes you are using. They can sense light, even when they are not consciously aware of it. And whilst their perspective of the vibrations of RGB may be very different between hand and eye, your ability to accurately translate baselines will enable you to recognise the amount of compensation needed.

Our consciousness is often referred to, in the study of psychology, as a *filter* through which our subconscious is played. Thus, our conscious mind is a minute fraction of the overall being. If we take this concept further, we see that the *conscious filter* is actually a synthesis of various parts; these parts being the aspects of our subconscious that are self-aware.

The synthesis or matrix acts as continuity, not only to give the individual a sense of self and wholeness, but also as a link from moment to moment. If we were a different person in each instant, we would have no idea who we were!

The conscious filter is therefore referred to by many as our ego or sense of self, yet is little more than an illusion, based upon other illusions. In fact, at any given point, our subconscious facets are jostling to be noticed by the conscious filter. Our consciousness can only work with a limited number of facets, so it favours those which offer *correct* data (this is usually information that is consistently backed up by experience over a period of time).

What our consciousness fails to realise is that as soon as a facet of our subconscious is connected into, it becomes real and therefore we will always see it as true. This can cause us challenges in PsyQ development, because we are used to dealing with fact, logic and the *real world*. So our consciousness ignores anything that conflicts with this unless we force it to listen.

This is why, in the initial stages of learning, we tend to question ourselves, what we are experiencing and our abilities. It is not that we cannot increase our PsyQ (or use a high PsyQ to achieve a multitude of results). It is that our consciousness is not used to working with PsyQ and needs to learn how to best leverage it.

Once we learn how to work with PsyQ, we realise the subconscious works very differently to our conscious mind. It does not, for the most part, use language. There are some facets of our subconscious that understand words, phrases or puns, but in the majority of cases, your subconscious will talk to you in tones, lights, images, dreams, daydreams, symbols and quick flashes of inspiration.

However, as you integrate the subconscious facets of yourself into the conscious filter/synthesis, you will find out how to translate the information into actual sensory features and very clear *cerebral* detail.

Conscious filter

Subconscious facets

So, whilst your consciousness is familiar with data received by the facet of your subconscious that decodes messages from your eyes, you may not see synaesthesia very well at the beginning of your training. However, as your subconscious decodes the living matrix, it will offer seemingly random and subtle experiences, such as flashes of light, *mind's eye* images, etc.

As you pay more attention to the living matrix facet of your subconscious, it will become just as real as your current visual information and experience.

Extrasensory perception refers to the use of senses beyond the traditional five senses of sight, hearing, smell, taste and touch. Often referred to as the *sixth sense*, we actually have many more.

Our living matrix accounts for various sensory layers that work with electromagnetic fields (EMF), extremely low-frequency vibrations (ELF) and other forms of subtle information such as scalar waves and pandimensional vibrations.

Nurturing our ESP abilities is relearning how to translate the sensory information that comes via the living matrix. The limiting beliefs we are exposed to as children often mean our ability to decipher the living matrix becomes atrophied and re-education is required to awaken this ability.

This process consists mainly of two elements: working through the other five senses and boosting the signal so that we can reach ever-increasing subtlety in the information we decode.

The first task is the equivalent of hearing a faraway whisper through a very loud and close scream. The sensory information that bombards your brain from your eyes alone is enough to scramble the living matrix communications from conscious recognition.

This initial phase requires the ability to focus only on the required levels of information, discounting the overwhelming stimuli that we are accustomed to. The key to this is to create stillness in all the other senses, either by closing them down (shutting your eyes) or preoccupying them with something else (a delicate smell or soft music).

Along with the autogenic training routine you are working with, the best way to calm and still the other senses, whilst enabling your mind to focus on the subtle vibrations of the living matrix is to alter your brain state (Appendix C).

For the specific purposes of perceiving this information through your traditional senses, alpha state is a wonderful place to be. Even better, theta state, which enhances your ability to read the extra-senses to a greater degree.

We can use the techniques here to change your brainwave state to the required degree. These techniques duplicate the logic behind autogenic training, inasmuch as you mimic the physiological results of the state you require, in order to create the desired reactions.

Your body cannot tell the difference between what you imagine to be happening and what is actually happening, so by accessing the regions of the brain that change the overall brainwave state, your body will automatically *click* into that state.

When using these techniques, the alpha state will frequently seem very subtle, because we naturally spend time in alpha at various points throughout the day. However, theta can be disorienting if you are not used to it, because it is the brain state linked with sleep, meditation and trance.

Triggering and concluding a theta session from/to wide awake may take some practice. Remember never to apply these techniques before/during driving, operating machinery or being in a position where you need to be alert or responsible for others.

Sit in a comfortable chair, where you will not be disturbed for a few minutes and close your eyes. With your eyes remaining closed, look up and twenty degrees to the right, as if staring at a clock face and looking to one o'clock.

Hold this eye position as you count down from a hundred to one in your head, each number counted with a two-second gap left in-between. When you finish this exercise you will be in alpha state.

If you discover during the exercise that your eyes have drifted away from the position, do not worry; just gently bring them back to twenty degrees. Additionally, if you lose track of the countdown, just return to the last number you remember.

The trick with this technique is not to try and relax, but to focus on what you are doing: on holding your eyes at twenty degrees and counting down. This stops you from being distracted by random thoughts, whilst your brain does the rest.

1. Sit comfortably, with your feet firmly on the floor, spine straight, eyes closed and shoulders relaxed.

2. Take several deep breaths, into your lower abdomen and expanding to the sides.

3. Clear your mind and focus only on your breathing, whilst you take your attention to the left hemisphere of your brain. Look up to the left for a moment and then pull your attention back into your head, until you reach the occipital region. Then move into the centre of your head and wait for a moment.

4. Take your attention to the right hemisphere of your brain. Look up to the right for a moment and then pull your attention back into your head, until you reach the occipital region.

5. Look up and to the left, then up and to the right. Return your eyes to the centre. Imagine your consciousness is moving backwards through your head. This is as if your attention is travelling in a vehicle which is driving backwards into the centre of your head.

6. Repeat several times.

7. Come back into the room.

Once you have mastered your ability to alter your brain state on command, it is time to focus on boosting the *volume* of the vibrations that travel through the living matrix, thus making them more perceptible.

We do this by increasing the amplitude of the vibrations; that is, *putting more energy into the quantum packets*. You can do this by using an energy cultivation technique or by using other vibrational exercises, including self-treatment, treatment of others, orientations and calibrations or practising Arena, etc.

We are all enveloped in and permeated by a subtle, bio-energetic field that is traditionally known as the auric field or aura. The aura is traditionally perceived as a range of vibrational energy that exists as various layers which extend away from the body.

It acts as a blueprint for the physical, emotional, mental and spiritual facets of the self and contains information about the person and their health, circumstances, thoughts and connections.

The aura not only reflects a person's health and state of being, but is also responsible for it. If something is changed in the aura, that change will ultimately filter through to the physical layers and become reflected in the person's body, emotions or thought patterns.

Every facet of the aura has a corresponding facet in the body. So, vibrations effect the physical body through the aura as part of three distinct systems (the aura, chakras and the meridian system).

Much has been written about the aura, detailing and extending ideas from the traditional beliefs of ancient Asian cultures, where the idea of an auric field originated. There has

The Auric Field

also been much questioning in recent years as to the nature of the aura from a scientific standpoint.

Most of these concepts and ideas can be read about in books, however, on this journey we shall go beyond the traditional and scientific beliefs and look at the auric field from a multidimensional perspective.

The basic traditions of the auric field are that it is comprised of four main degrees of energy: the etheric, emotional, mental and spiritual. There are additional subdivisions that differ, depending on the methodology used. Each layer is linked to specific areas of the physical being; affecting and affected by those areas.

When we examine the auric field in a scientific way, we see that the field of energy surrounding the body is merely a collection of differing ELF vibrations that reaches beyond the ability of even the most modern sensory equipment.

However, if we then look to the most advanced scientific research we begin to comprehend an even more amazing phenomenon—a quanta is not found in one place; it is found in every possible place! Therefore, regardless of where the energy of our auric field originates, it exists at every possible point in the universe.

The word *possible* is of paramount importance when considering the aura, as it limits the *carte blanche* range of auric vibrations. For instance, if we look at the energy emitted from the physical body; there is a connection between the body and the vibrations, so the energy can only exist (in this form) where it is possible to be connected to the body.

The fact that your physical form could not survive in the depths of space or the centre of the earth, means that the vibrations cannot be there either—however, wherever it is possible for your body to go, your physically connected auric energy can go also.

If we consider that your body contains genetic material that has been passed to you across millions of years, we see that not only do you have access to millions of years of experience, but it is also possible for these vibrations of energy to be at any point in that expanse of time!

When we apply the same principles to the energetic fields created by thought processes, we see that virtually anything becomes possible!

With this change of perspective, we realise that, just as the quanta of energy are connected to us, we are connected to those quanta. This denotes that our aura is an infinite array of connections, not only to the physical, but to the non-physical too: an energetic time machine, which only requires the switching of state to transport us to any possible place and time.

Of course, this shift is merely energetic, so you do not physically transport back to the Tudor period or the age of the dinosaurs, but energetically you can. This means that the information from those times is also available to us.

We shall measure the impact of this later, but for now, let us turn to the subject of personal readings. What we are aiming to achieve in any reading is to pinpoint the connection that your client is consciously aware of (their perspective of energy).

From that point we can surmise where that *path* will lead them. We can also offer them alternatives and help them to connect into vibrations that are more conducive for them, whatever those may be.

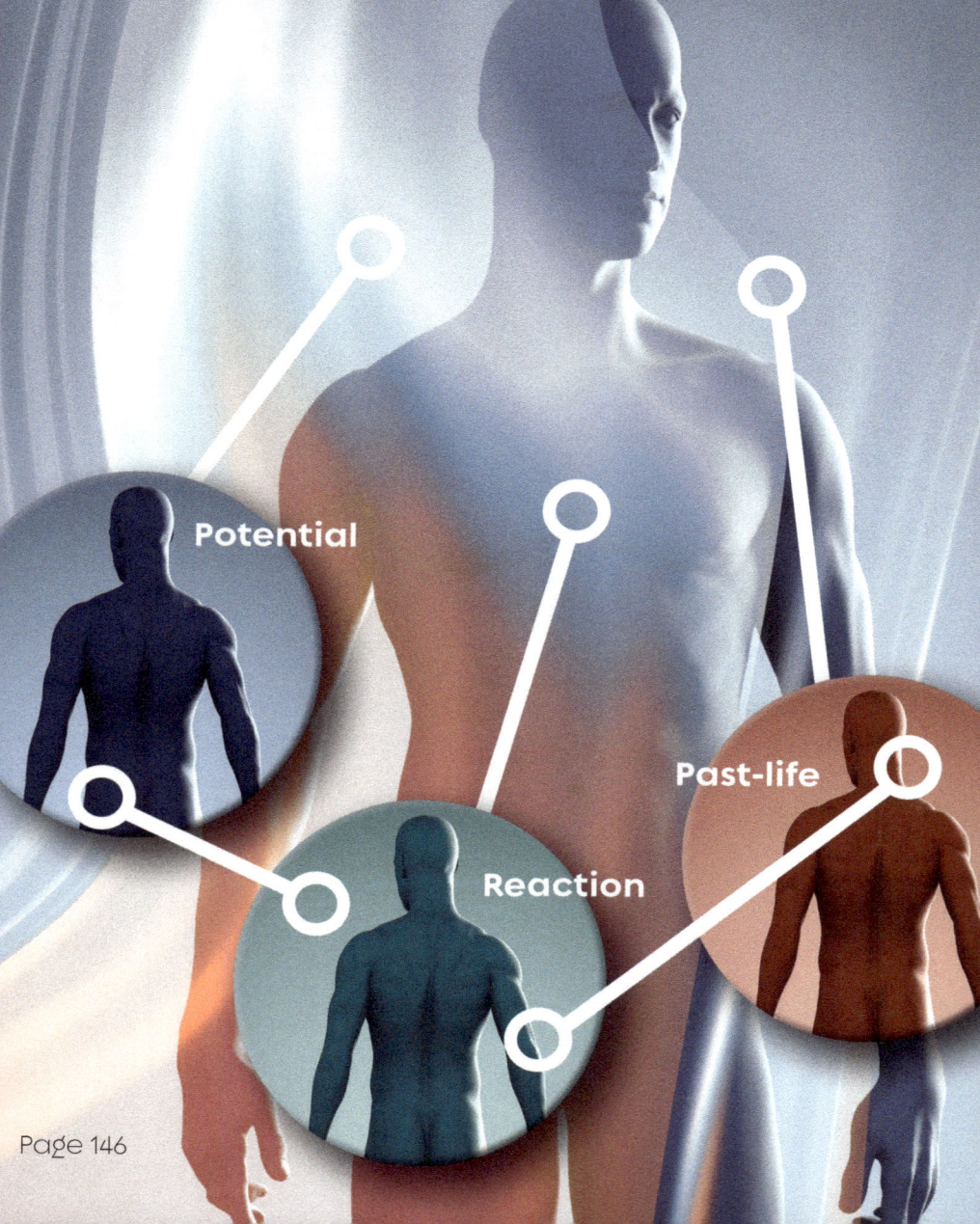

The Processes of Personal Readings

Whilst the art of personal readings is a specialist form of PsyQ work that can require a huge body of experience to master, it also spans many different fields, including psychic and therapy work. When we can read the subtle waves of energy associated with the body or beyond, we can discover a whole range of information about a person.

The process involved in reading these vibrations and translating them into valuable feedback for your client is only half the story however, as we also require the skills associated with client care, ethical considerations and how to conduct a professional consultation. As there are no specific regulations for PsyQ work at present, these factors are guidelines rather than laws. It is still essential, however, that we work to improve overall standards in the field and set a benchmark for PsyQ consultants everywhere.

The Philosophy of Personal Readings

There are three subdivisions of personal readings that we shall be investigating in this Home Experience: physical readings, which pertain to the reading of mind, body emotions and social circumstances; PsyQ readings, which offer a link to other intelligences, beyond the human and finally the past life readings that we shall explore later.

All personal readings work on the foundation of one simple philosophy—we read vibrations and translate those vibrations into feedback for our clients.

The differences occur when we distinguish which vibrations we focus on and the logic we use in the translation process. So, for example, when we conduct a physical reading, we are looking at the vibrations emitted from our client's physiological functions and brainwave patterns.

A PsyQ reading focuses on energetic patterns that are not directly connected to the client's body/mind, but are traditionally viewed as *external* to the client.

There is an inconceivable array of energetic vibrations for us to work with, from the vibrations of the physical body, the chemicals that form our emotions and our thought patterns, to the vast range of EMF/ELF fields that surround and pervade us. The more physical a vibration, the easier it is to sense. So, by starting with the EMF fields from electronic equipment, we can move on to the more subtle waveforms of the living body.

As we evolve through each layer, increasing our sensitivity to a greater degree of intricacy, we discover the finer nuances of vibration and become more *energetic*. There are no limits as to how far we can expand our PsyQ abilities, except those we place on ourselves either consciously or subconsciously.

Let us begin with physical readings and examine what we are focusing upon when we work with a client.

Our bodies are amazing machines, which consist of complex interactions and processes. These are present in all of us, so can be easily recognised if we simply take a moment to acknowledge their existence.

We are an encyclopaedia of experience, from the huge array of electrical information that is present in the brain, to the chemical interactions that communicate our feelings on a cell-to-cell basis.

Some of us have retained, from childhood, a natural ability to distinguish these complex dynamics and interpret what they mean. We often refer to these individuals as empathic or having a high PsyQ.

However, the majority of people in the Western world have been taught how not to sense, so they may understand there to be *something*, but are unable to explain what that might be. The fact is that we can all sense this information—it is just a matter of recognising it!

Once you have established a connection to your client's physiological state, you then need to make allowances for perspective. The fact that we are all unique means one person may react to certain dynamics in a way which is completely different from our own personal reactions. For example, if you read a high level of adrenalin in the bloodstream, you may subconsciously interpret your client's reaction to be identical to your own reaction to the same substance.

However, if too much adrenalin causes you to feel stressed, anxious and gives you palpitations, these are what you will feel in the reading. If your client thrives on adrenalin, using it to motivate them to get things done, your reading will be inaccurate. Thus, we require a change of perspective: an energetic filter with which we can convert our client's responses into our own.

The reading begins with an orientation and calibration to our client's perspective. Remembering that we only ever retain our own, personal perspective of our client's perspective, we then set about altering our state of mind so that we can read the vibrations we sense. These vibrations, in both categories of personal readings, are contained within the auric field and can be accessed by focusing on the relevant facets of energy.

At this point we see that when you access the energetic information of your client's auric field, you have an infinite range of possibility, so you are aiming directly for the facets of energy that form your client's conscious connections: their perspective. When you connect here, you can then extrapolate what is likely to happen (forecast/prediction) and suggest alternatives—as you make these suggestions, you enable your client's awareness to connect to those possible futures and give them choices.

When we move to the analysis of PsyQ readings, we shift our attention to experiences that are beyond human and require an explanation of what we mean by this. We also need to appreciate how to associate this appreciation to the conduct of personal readings.

Here we encounter a vast and complex range of vibrational experiences, we cannot easily describe these in a few sentences. Instead, we need to isolate the range of experiences involved, particularly in personal readings.

In the practice of physical readings, we focus on the facets of energy that originate from connection to the body/mind of a person. When working with PsyQ readings, however, we tend to look for the vibrations connected directly to an aspect of experience that is beyond human.

Whenever we work with a subject that encompasses a person's integral beliefs and spiritual perspective, we always need to broach the subject with sensitivity and a deep respect for their views.

Here, we need to possess an adaptable, yet powerful range of knowledge and techniques, whilst also respecting the beliefs and spiritual perspective of everybody in the realms. The challenge is many tend to automatically equate a vibrational experience with a traditional ethos. This may work for them, but not for everybody.

The vibrations of an intelligence, beyond the physical human experience, will often be labelled a ghost. But a ghost is a very specific religious concept, as are guides, angels and demons. Strip away the labels and you have the potential for so much more. Here, we shall look at the practical, rather than the theological, so you can adapt your journey to fit into your own beliefs.

We now embark on a topic that overlaps some of the sensitive areas as we need to explore how these *reading tools* came about. I have worked with many sensitives and PsyQ consultants over the years and have made a particular point of perceiving the underlying processes of what we do (it is difficult to do this on oneself, so I have restricted my research to other people).

The following description specifies the experiences during personal readings. It does not account for personal beliefs, but is based upon what is perceptively happening vibrationally during a reading, regardless of the individual's beliefs (Spiritualist, Eastern, Occultist, Shamanic and so on).

My speciality is energy work so I tend towards the dynamics of the process. In describing those dynamics, I seek to give a non-denominational portrait of the inner workings, which can also be adapted for your own use, whatever your personal faith.

This is the essence of a person or some other guiding or mentoring intelligence. In traditional terms we are focusing on ghosts, spirits or guides. However, this essence is not another person as they were in life, but an essential spark of that person; the qualities that the client perceived in a client's relative or more appropriately, wanted to perceive.

Where *guides* and mentors are perceived in the auric field, these can be seen as *potentials*: what it is viable for a person to become if they work towards their bliss or joy.

Every moment of experience is part of the matrix that forms our auric field and those moments that are shared with others are present in essence also. Our perspective of those essences is important, because to see a specific essence as *contractive*, means we will resist it and create contractive dynamics from it. If we perceive an essence as expansive, we open ourselves up to the potential and possibility of all that can be achieved.

To somebody who had a loving grandmother, they will live (in essence) as part of a person's auric field, forever a source of inspiration and joy. An abusive uncle will be a constant reminder of fear and dejection, yet, if they can be repatterned so a person's feelings towards them are neutral or even expansive they create a much healthier dynamic.

Does this mean that we have to accept even the most heinous behaviour?

No, because the vibrations of the auric field are connected to you and therefore can be seen as your vibrations—you are forgiving yourself, rather than accepting the behaviour of the person who has hurt you.

Potentials exist in the auric field (as sentient beings), because the auric field of a person in the future (who they will become) is in every possible point in the universe. As long as it is possible for a person to achieve that future, it is possible for that specific facet of energy to exist now.

By connecting to that facet of energy, the potential can guide the person closer to that possible outcome and help them to fulfil their hopes and dreams.

When you, as a PsyQ consultant, connect to those facets of energy, you want to integrate them as closely to your client's perspective as possible, so that they can also know who you are talking about.

Once you have done this, the wealth of information that can be gleaned from that connection will provide an accurate and helpful reading for your client. Do be aware, however, that on occasion, you may make a secondary or even tertiary connection, which is where you connect to the experience of one relative, via the perspective of another relative.

Say, for example, your client has a definite picture in their mind, of who their grandfather was; yet you connect to a message for your client's grandmother (from her husband). You would perceive your client's grandfather through the energetic filter of your perspective of your client's perspective, of your client's grandmother's perspective, of your client's grandfather! Confusing?

In this instance it is quite possible to see your client's grandfather as a young, attractive man, just as your client's grandmother remembers him. It is very possible that your client may not even recognise who he is!

Every person works in their own unique way, so it down to you to unravel how you perceive energy and gather the various signs as to what facet of energy you are working with, what the connection is and why this has come to the surface.

There is one way of doing this—practise! However, believe in yourself; it is remarkable how quickly we learn and how much knowledge we accumulate in a very short time!

Here are three different facets of energy we can use to prime and receive information. The first acts as a means of connecting you to those aspects of the aura that pertain to physical readings, with a second, similar facet for PsyQ readings. The third facet boosts the information received so that it is easier to sense and translate into usable feedback for your client.

The triggers for these facets of energy are:

Physical Prime,

PsyQ Prime and

Enhance.

To activate each facet, simply say the trigger three times, in your head.

The practical routine of conducting a reading also differs between the physical and PsyQ varieties. Whilst these can be conducted as a series of steps, for training purposes, the practice is an art form that you will tailor and adapt over time.

As you gain confidence and experience, you will make the readings as individual as the client you are working with and discover a greater accuracy and depth to the information you receive.

PHYSICAL READINGS TECHNIQUE

1. Sit at an angle to your client and take a few moments to orientate towards their auric field. At any time during the reading, pay attention to information that pops into your head and say this out loud.

2. Once you have felt a shift to their perspective, activate the *Physical-Prime*-triggered facet of energy and project this using the direct or distance methods.

The Practice of Personal Readings

3. When you feel the second shift, switch to the *Enhance* trigger and then use distance/direction projection.

4. Now use distance or direct reception to gather the information and start to detail all information out loud, rather than internally.

PSYQ READINGS TECHNIQUE

1. Sit at an angle to your client and, once again, take a while to orientate towards their auric field. Remember to mention anything that comes to you at all times throughout the reading.

2. Once you have felt a shift to their perspective, activate the *PsyQ-Prime*-triggered facet of energy and project this using the direct or distance methods.

3. Start to become aware of any presence, figure or shift in feeling of the room/location.

4. Switch to the *Enhance* trigger, using distance/direct projection.

5. Now use distance or direct reception from the area of the presence, figure or energy shift to gather information and start to detail all information out loud, rather than internally. If you are able to receive from the vibrational area (frequency) rather than the physical area (space), this will be more effective.

The Profession of Personal Readings

When working as a professional PsyQ consultant, we balance our art with the practicalities of professional conduct, including ethics and the law. It is very important to remember these aspects of your practice, not only for the wellbeing of your clients, but also for your own peace of mind.

Maintaining a professional environment and practice means that you can enjoy your art, without falling prey to some of the common oversights made by many professionals. By knowing the boundaries, you can be free to enjoy your art within those boundaries and liberate yourself from much of the dogma that has infiltrated our industry.

The ethical factors of PsyQ work can be complex and are usually driven by perspective and debate, however we shall look at some of the main issues later in this section. For the moment, let us explore the less ambiguous area of the law and the legalities of practice.

The law differs from territory to territory, so it is important to research the specific laws of your country or state.

PsyQ Readings and the Law

Diagnosis—if ever you pick up a medical condition in your client's reading, you must never diagnose, unless you are qualified to do so. Diagnosing a dis-ease or condition may lead to legal action, even if the diagnosis is correct! If you are concerned about your client, ask them if they have had any *issues* with the area in question and, if they have, refer them to their GP.

Hospitals—Never undertake PsyQ readings or treatments in hospital without permission from the ward staff first. Even if you have permission, you should wait to be asked by patients, rather than offering your services. A good way to do this is to wear a badge, saying that you offer PsyQ readings/treatments.

Authority—Never contradict the advice of a doctor or medical consultant. If you have any doubts about offering readings or treatments, ask your client to provide a signed document from their doctor to say that they have no objections to reading/treatment.

Client Confidence—You have an obligation to your client to maintain their confidence regarding personal details and consultation feedback. However, it is the law that if you keep your client's details on a computer, you must abide by the relevant Data Protection Act and cannot release their details to other parties.

It is also a legal requirement that if your client confides illegal activities of a serious nature (past or planned), you must report these to the police—it is of course open to debate, what constitutes a *serious nature*.

You are also required to notify a person's doctor if they state they are intending to harm themselves or others. Remember these must be statements made by the client—your intuition and the information gleaned from it, falls into the ethics category, rather than being governed by the law!

Insurance—You may not be not required by law to have insurance for readings, events or even treatments, but it will help your professional standing if you have an appropriate PI insurance policy and many PsyQ event organisers insist that you have insurance.

The Ethics of PsyQ Readings

The ethical debates that surround PsyQ work are numerous and tend to boil down to the view of each personal PsyQ consultant. Without official regulations, the majority of reading work comes down to opinion and personal choice.

For example, the boundaries of what and what not to tell clients—do you express good and bad news or to you try to soften any painful information? How about a situation where you connect to information about a crime or abusive relationship? Some PsyQ consultants would remain impartial, whilst others would try to intervene in the situation.

Another debate is what to advise people about their beliefs, habits or choices especially when these involve circumstances that you do not agree with. Many PsyQ consultants, for instance, object strongly to the use of Ouija boards and offer the advice that they are dangerous, whilst others will criticise their clients for religious belief or spiritual practices.

Do be aware that we are working with individuals who have their own perspectives. They will often look upon you as somebody who is in authority or is wiser than they are. Everything you say has the potential to change lives and create major dynamics for people.

When it comes to the ethical/moral debate in readings and consultations, we have to make our choices about what we say and how we act. Often the best standpoint to take is that of perspective—if you can speak in your client's terms, using their phraseology and conceptual outlook, you will become more ethical without thinking about it. As you naturally connect to your clients you are more likely to understand what will hurt and what will inspire.

Remember that expansive polarity words will also help you to give advice in a way that motivates and creates an optimistic outlook. If you can keep your linguistic approach expansive, you will not only avoid difficult questions, but will also keep others in an optimistic frame of mind.

When it comes to how you act when confronted with an ethical question that requires some form of definite action, the responsibility is with you and your own beliefs—here, the best thing to do is to be true to yourself...

The Karmic/ Miasmatic Perspective

We now turn our attention to the past life reading, which can be viewed from two different perspectives: that of karma and the Eastern philosophies or the miasmatic view of Western complementary therapies.

The belief in karma has foundations in the ancient Far East, with the priests and energy workers in the sacred temples from Japan to Tibet. It was in the religious beliefs of these priests that we see the concept of karma most clearly and it is here we understand that the energetic soul embarks on a path through many lives so that it may gather wisdom and reach an enlightened state of being.

On a soul's journey it encounters many contrasting and sometimes conflicting circumstances. Depending on how the soul acts and reacts to these events, it creates karma. Painful karma is when a soul abuses another and enlightenment karma is when a soul is compassionate to another. Every action that the soul takes creates karma of some form and this is then *bounced back* to the soul, sometimes during a single life, sometimes over many.

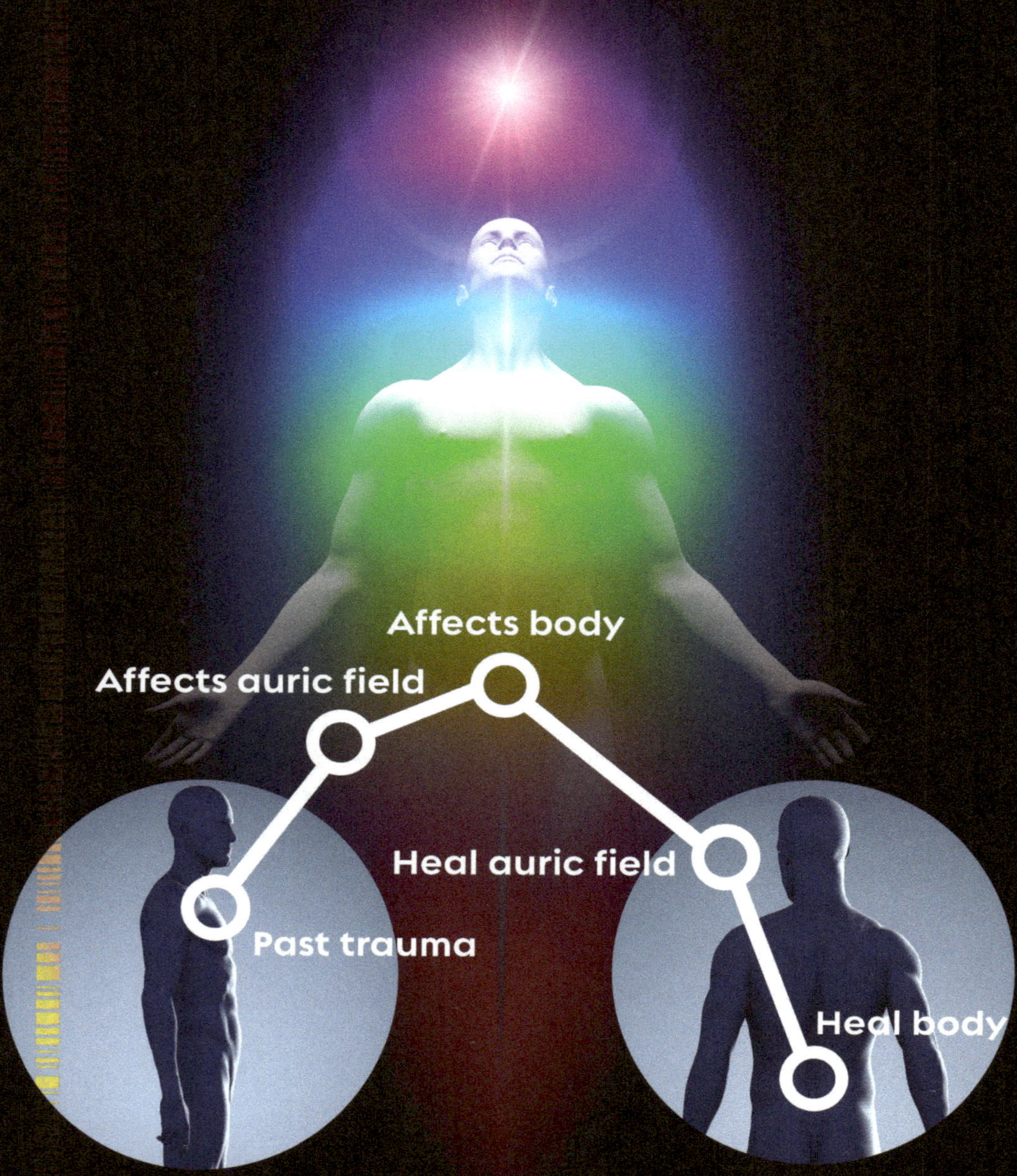

Affects body

Affects auric field

Heal auric field

Past trauma

Heal body

This process translates differently depending on the particular faith you are working with, so in some traditions your karma decides whether you progress to the next level of enlightenment or stray to lower, less enlightened planes of being.

In other, more extreme belief systems, we see that if you are cruel in your current life, you shall be reincarnated as the person or animal you have been cruel to!

If you have *good* karma you will attract good things, *bad* karma thus creates bad influences—or so the tradition says. It is always wise to remember that the concepts of good and bad are relative, what was bad two-hundred years ago is often not seen as bad now, whereas perfectly acceptable customs then may be abhorrent in today's society!

When we switch to the miasmatic view of past lives, we understand that the energetic soul takes the form of vibrations at a genetic level, which is passed down from parents to child. These vibrations contain the memories of trauma and dis-ease, which affect the way that we function in this life.

With each lifetime, the vibrations become more diluted and paradoxically stronger. Therefore the older the miasm, the greater its effect will be for each new generation of individuals. As we clear these *memories*, it is believed that we become *purer*, healthier and more enlightened. Thus we see that vibrations pass from life to life and the actions contained in each life affect the next.

The approach you take is entirely up to you; the romantic notion of karma can be a huge comfort to people, yet the miasmatic view is much more appropriate for the logically minded, who find no solace in a life they cannot remember.

In addition to this, be aware that in a karmic perspective, it is easier to relinquish blame—"I was a mass-murderer in a past life, so I deserve a bad time in this one." Whereas a miasmatic standpoint brings responsibility to overcome each *miasm* in the present, leaving it with the living individual to work with.

With both the karmic and miasmatic views, the vibrations from lives, previous to the current one, are contained in the auric field (and other energy systems). These vibrations enable us to directly access the life or situation and therefore create a direct solution.

We can sense and interpret every vibration into *objects*, such as tastes, smells, sights, sounds and shapes. Once we have been able to sense the vibrations of energy, your subconscious mind will translate these sensations into usable, conscious information.

At first this information may take the form of strange tones in your ears, flashing lights/dark patches before the eyes, tingling, shaking, vibrating, heat and other feelings, etc.

Over time, however, you will find more sophisticated messages come through and this will eventually become tangible images and information about karmic connections. You will also be able to pick up on ancestral information and the karmic/historical connection of places and buildings.

The purpose of past life readings is to glean imagery and information, which can offer a link to the current situation of the client. So if they have life or health issues, which they are finding difficult to solve, a karmic/miasmatic reading can often provide an alternative perspective, which can then help to reveal different methods of approach.

What you will tend to find when doing past life readings, is that simple objects will gradually turn into complex stories, with elaborate situations and details. These can offer an extremely valuable insight into what is happening in even the most bizarre situation and present practical advice on how to overcome the most deep-rooted of issues.

Remember that we have a direct energetic link to the traumas of past lives in our auric field; we will have corresponding traumas in our bodies. Clear the trauma from the aura and the body's vibrations will follow. By focusing your client's attention on the issue and offering advice on how to clear it, we can assist them in the repatterning/clearing process.

So let us explore the techniques and tools we use when conducting a past life reading for a client, starting with the facets of energy, which you would have learned in the orientation and calibration in the realms.

THE PRIMER ENERGY—
TRIGGER NAME: "PAST LIFE PRIME", SAID THREE TIMES.

This facet of energy is projected into your connection to the auric field to prime it for treatment. By doing so, primer increases the vibrations contained in the aura and starts to shake loose any karmic vibrations for you to work with.

The primer also helps your PsyQ abilities to activate, specifically in the range of karmic/miasmatic work and can ease the ability to translate the subconscious sensing of energy into conscious information.

THE SENSING ENERGY—
TRIGGER NAME: "PAST LIFE SENSE", SAID THREE TIMES.

The *sensing energy* is the main tool of our past life reading as it is this range of vibrations that helps you to sense what is happening in your client's auric field. Increasing the amplitude of the karmic vibrations makes them easier to sense. It also works over a period of time to increase your sensitivity and understanding of karmic/miasmatic vibrations of energy.

In addition to the energy we use in a reading, we also have sensory tools to help us intuit the energy of the aura. These tools consist of sight, sound, smell, taste and most importantly hand movements that enable us to feel past life events in a tangible form.

We can interpret the vibrational information as movement, allowing our hands to bounce and flow along the various patterns we encounter. These flows offer us sensory representations of the objects and situations we encountered in our clients' past lives and are often accompanied with images, sounds and other sensory data.

So, if you were treating a person who had been hung in a previous life, you may well interpret this information as an energetic noose around their neck. This scenario is actually very common and people are often amazed as they see their hands *stroke* the rope of the noose, complete with their fingers bouncing over the bumps in the rope.

By working with the flows and bounce of this experience we sensitise our hands to the vibrations and therefore to the information contained within. As we learn to sense the information, our living matrix becomes more adept at feeling the energy and soon you will discover that you no longer need to use your hands, because your other senses will take over!

PAST LIFE READINGS TECHNIQUE

1. Sit at an angle to your client and take a moment to orientate towards their auric field. Ask your client to close their eyes for a moment, to relax and clear their mind. Remember to mention anything that comes to you at all times throughout the reading.

2. Once you have felt a shift to their perspective, activate the *Past-Life-Prime*-triggered facet of energy and project this using the direct or distance methods.

3. Close your eyes and activate theta state. Then, keeping your shoulders relaxed, lift your arms at the elbow and allow them to hang above your lap. If your hands start to move, let this happen also.

4. Switch to the *Past Life Sense* trigger, using either distance or direct projection.

5. Now open your eyes and sense the flow and bounce of your client's aura, as your hands move ask questions about what you are sensing and say out loud (whilst training) the answers you receive.

6. Once you have enough information come back into the room, ask your client to open their eyes and discuss your discoveries with them.

Chapter Summary

To reach the required level of knowledge for this region of the Home Experience, you will need to:

Do You Know?

Have a basic understanding of the following methods/terms:

- Alpha/theta state
- Passive/active prediction methods
- EMF, ELF, ESP
- Karmic/miasmatic perspectives
- Primer and sense facets of energy

Understand the importance of personal readings in connection to other forms of PsyQ activity, such as communication with potentials.

Be aware of the importance of perspective in personal readings, ESP and all vibrational work, including the reasons that initial testing is not conducive to development.

Detail the workings of the auric field in a modern perspective, including direct energetic connections between the aura and other circumstances, situations, places and times (states of energy).

- Be able to activate alpha state
- Be able to activate theta state
- Be able to carry out sensory work on different people
- Be able to conduct a physical reading (at least in theory)
- Be able to conduct a PsyQ reading (at least in theory)
- Be able to conduct a karmic/miasmatic reading (at least in theory)

Learn and be able to describe how chemical/cellular communication works, including a description of neurochemicals, opiate receptors and receptor bundles.

Describe the concept of hydrogen bonding and grasp the importance of this when considering vibrational effects on the body and mind. Speculate how hydrogen bonding could be responsible for miasmatic aspects of a person and introduce the idea that connection to certain vibrations may cause an emotional response.

Chapter Homework & Exercises

ONE: ALPHA AND THETA STATES

Practise activating alpha and theta states once a day. These should be done at separate times, perhaps in the morning after waking and at night before bed. If possible, these should be done before the AT routine.

TWO: SENSING PEOPLE

As you interact with other people on an everyday basis, attempt to sense their energy fields, with your sight, hearing or hands. Try to find words to describe anything you sense. Orientate yourself to their perspective and then come back to your own perspective—jot down how this feels and any interesting results you find.

THREE: READING PEOPLE

If you know people who are willing to act as practice partners conduct a physical, personal and karmic reading on each partner. If you do not have people who will help out, try conducting readings on the people about you, at work, on buses/trains, in the queue at the post office, anywhere you have the opportunity. Focus particularly on the different feel and effects of individuals.

Four: Continuations from Chapter One

Continue to work with your linguistic approach, monitoring the words that you use in connection with yourself and your PsyQ practices. Conduct self-treatments when required, and continue to conduct and add to your AT routine, listed in the additional notes. Finally, continue your breathing exercises, either separately or as part of other practices.

Five: RGB Entrainment

Work with the red/green/blue entrainment exercise. Activate each colour in turn and try to sense the vibrations triggered. The closer you can get the appropriate colours to appear before your closed eyes or in your mind's eye, the better this will be for your ability to attune to other perspectives.

Rescue work is one of the most rewarding and profound branches of PsyQ. It spans a wide variety of different, yet similar areas. Traditionally given labels as emotive as *exorcism* and *banishment of the disincarnate*, these specialist PsyQ activities are a common theme in popular culture—yet are often viewed with scepticism or puzzlement.

In Christian culture it was believed that the soul of the dead either travelled to heaven or to hell. If a soul could not find its way and did not make this transition, it would become stuck between worlds, destined to walk alone until helped or rescued from its fate. This help would usually take the form of a priest, although in later years psychic practitioners have also undertaken the role of assisting the *lost souls* who roam the earth.

As times and cultural attitudes changed, having incorporated new ideas from other faiths, spiritualities and science (now the most popular spirituality in the West), we have moved beyond this concept.

Yet, simply because we have changed in our minds, does it mean the lost stopped being lost?

Our ancestors believed in a limbo and those who walked there—did our own evolution cause them all to find their way home?

The shift in perspective was ours and so it is down to us to recreate the link that connects us to those who, for whatever reason, remain lost.

Now some may ask why we need to do rescue work when we have so many other things to deal with in our own lives. If they are not bothering us, then why should we bother them? But they do bother us; they are still lost and they cannot find peace. What makes this even more integral to who we are is, until we help them to find their rest, we are unable to find ours.

Here, we shall be drawing on the philosophies covered previously and examining an original way of identifying with rescue work. We investigate how our energetic perspective of PsyQ development leads us to understand an inherent bond to the intelligences that exist beyond ourselves.

This bond suggests that we only ever come into contact with those whom we share associations. Through this connection we discover more about who we are than we ever thought possible.

From this alternate perspective we shall use our healing tool kit to create an *energetic rescue kit* that consists of various techniques and *essences* to assist you with a multitude of situations and circumstances.

This kit will form a basis for helping the lost whenever you encounter them and whatever their needs may be.

The Ties That Bind

Everything that exists is created at an integral level from energy—energy is infinite. We are all connected by this common thread that runs through all things and when you truly grasp this concept, you realise there is no separation apart from the illusion that physical space creates.

In all this infinite energy, each one of us is merely a point of perspective: a state of energy from which everything else is witnessed. In our physical world we experience energy in solid form, with all the joy and sorrows that brings. We go through our lives, learning and experiencing as if it was the first time. We see wonderment and pain and we evolve. However, in a vast incomprehensible universe, at what point do we stop being a physical being and start being something else?

People are only aware of what lies within their own sphere of perception. So if you are only working from your physical sphere, you will only ever notice, at a conscious level, your physical world and day-to-day life.

By expanding the sphere to incorporate expanded experiences of energy you notice the subtle layers of ELF and transpersonal intelligence. Everything that exists beyond your sphere of perception will also be outside your conscious awareness.

This equates to energy beyond our sphere as being *something else* and, as such, other people/beings and everything external falls outside of our sphere. Yet, we can perceive other people and the world around us, so how can these be external to our sphere of perception?

We may be aware that other beings exist, both physically and ethereally. How can we explain this?

Every person we are aware of exists outside of our perception, although every aspect of those people that we consciously experience also exists inside of our sphere. This denotes that some facet of energy that is within their sphere is also within our sphere.

We share the same vibrations of energy, like a reflection in a mirror. This also means that every single person that you have ever been aware of in your life shares certain vibrations with you. This is the case whether a person is seen as a loved one or somebody who has been cruel; whether they have offered you kindness and friendship or grief and pain.

The greater the similarity in energetic patterns, the closer you will feel towards the person or the more they will haunt you. As we grow and evolve through experience, we alter our facets of energy and so people come into and go out of our lives. The constant ebb and flow is only matched by how we also stay the same in other aspects and can thus form lifelong bonds or karma.

In the study of metaphysical practices, it is said that every person we meet reflects our own qualities back to us. They do this to show us ourselves in a way that we cannot understand or realise on our own.

These ties between people are what shape our lives and offer us the dynamics by which we grow and become who we are. Without them, we would simply be energy—knowing all there is to know except what it feels like not to know.

So this explains people, but what about the other elements of our lives? What about animals: do we share energy with them?

According to the indigenous shamans of North America, the animals we encounter in our life display innate qualities within us. A totem creature possesses a form of energy that also exists within the individual person. For example the wolf (who is a teacher) and the alligator (who displays the balance between thought and emotion).

Now, even if we can debate how all living things share energy, what about a table, a chair, the homes we live in or even the locations of those homes… do we really share vibrations with these inanimate objects?

If we travel to ancient China and the practices of *feng shui,* we see that our homes and the items contained within, not only reflect, but also play an active part in the way our lives develop and flow.

The Huna beliefs of Hawaii say that we *reflect our inner state of being* outwardly in the way we decorate and arrange our homes. A loft jam-packed with junk will tell of a person whose head is filled with too much to think about, while a basement or storage areas that are in disrepair display somebody who is neglecting the health of their body and so on.

Everything in our life reflects some form of connection or energetic bond that we have, just beyond our perception. By recognising these bonds, we learn the vibrations from which they are created and are therefore able to work directly with that particular variety of energy.

The identification of a specific facet of energy within our sphere translates to either a sense of self-love and fulfilment, when we recognise that facet as being one of expansive reaction, or the need to heal and repattern if it causes painful, contractive responses.

Hence, when we encounter a pattern of energy that is just within our sphere of perception, but that we do not identify with, it causes us to fear it rather than embrace and heal it. When we consider just how many energetic patterns exist in our ancestry alone that are repressive, oppressive and traumatic, we see that at subtle and hidden layers of our being there is much to incorporate and repattern.

We reflect
what is inside,
outside

And by healing
what we reflect
in the world...

We heal
what is inside

The process of understanding and healing contractive-response energy is done completely naturally and, as long as we do not suppress the process, without us even having to think about it.

The problem is that as we start to perceive the energetic patterns that appear upon the limits of our perception, we recognise them within ourselves and it is these vibrations that cause us to feel horrible. Energetic vibrations that have no connection to you and thus are not a part of you, cannot affect you.

To understand this better, think about what happens if you eat something that is toxic to your body; your body will attempt to get rid of the noxious substance by inducing vomiting. It is not the thing you have eaten that is causing you to be sick—it is your body reacting to the toxin.

Additionally, if you have a virus, your body will heat up to try and wipe the virus out, hence the virus is not creating the temperature; your body is. Exactly the same thing happens with the energetic patterns we encounter: your body recognises them within your vibrations and attempts to repattern them—as this process takes place, we sense the reaction and externalise it.

At every moment of every day, your brain is functioning with an infinite array of connections and encounters. The vibrations your brain has no awareness of are completely dismissed without any acknowledgement at all.

The vibrations you are familiar with might infiltrate your awareness, but your brain will still pay little attention to these because you understand everyday vibrations to be of no consequence to your consciousness. Accordingly, the facets of energy you are accustomed to will usually be processed subconsciously.

Yet, when you come into contact with vibrations that you have suppressed or that lie hidden at deep-seated levels of your being, your body may try to reject these. It is this reaction that focuses your conscious mind very sharply on those vibrations.

Of course it is habitual and instinctual that you perceive these vibrations to be the cause of a contractive reaction, so you try to push them away or bury them deeper. When we understand that the reaction of our body to the vibrations is a healing one, we are more likely to embrace those facets that cause us to feel disagreeable. We understand that by working with the sensations rather than rejecting them, we are enabling the body to learn and so overcome the detrimental effects of those vibrations.

Some people opt to do this particular journey through physical illness, whilst others reflect their challenges into the situations they encounter. Others take a healing path while some choose PsyQ development; in particular, rescue work.

Each and every time we help the lost to heal, we heal ourselves in the process. This is why rescue work is so profound and such a beautifully orchestrated opus—by helping fragmented and discordant experiences of consciousness, we create an intense process of healing and all who encounter it are brought into the light.

Energy is infinite and timeless, yet our perception of it is played through physical space and on a timeline of history. You treat each energetic state and facet you encounter from your unique perspective and place it on to a linear path that stretches out behind you.

This path began at the very beginning of space and time and will continue to be constructed until the end of time and space. However, until you have lived a particular state or facet, it is not part of your path even if you are aware of its existence.

Sometimes we give a facet of energy the chance to consciously experience physicality and recreate its particular dynamic in our own lives, thus making it part of our own path of experience. So if you are aware of intense physical pain at a subliminal level (which most of us are), you may choose to experience that intense pain in the form of a broken leg.

As soon as you experience the events in which your leg becomes broken, it is a part of your path and the subsequent healing process that you undergo not only heals the broken leg, it enables you to repattern the connection you have to the energetic facet of intense pain.

The Hypothesis of Healing Connections

Conversely, if you are able to experience that same dynamic through the eyes of another person, you can learn how they healed themselves and use their perspective as a basis for your own healing. In doing so, you need never connect to the broken leg experience or similar. We can also work through this progression by working directly with energy in the form of lost and fragmented forms of intelligence.

If you help to release the experience of a person who was tortured in their lifetime, you become aware of how (energetically) they transcended the experience of being tortured and all the related connections. You can thus use their experience to repattern your own energetic facets accordingly and never need experience the actual trauma resulting from the torture dynamic played out in your path of experience.

Be aware that an energetic dynamic, such as *torture*, does not necessarily manifest as actual torture; it might be a painful experience or some form of abuse, for example. Let us look at this concept in the form of a hypothetical case study that spans several lifetimes and energetic connections…

The Story of Margaret

Margaret lives in a London suburb at the beginning of the twentieth century, when she meets and falls in love with Henry. They begin courting and eventually choose to get engaged; it is the highpoint of Margaret's life when Henry asks her to marry him and she knows that she has met the man of her dreams; her soulmate.

When war is declared between Britain and Germany, it is not long before the couple are separated after Henry is called up to serve in the army. After months of correspondence via letter, Margaret receives the news that she has been dreading—Henry has been killed.

It takes Margaret many years to come to terms with her loss. Her grief during that time is almost unbearable. Yet, she finally heals herself and then meets her would-be husband, before settling down and having two beautiful children. She always keeps Henry in her heart and never forgets her love for him and while the hurt is healed, it always exists on some level, existing vibrationally through the years, even after her death.

The Story of David

David is born many years after her death. In miasmatic terms he is her great, great grandson. Deep within David's energetic perspective there remains Margaret's pain and grief, which he is aware of on a subliminal level, but this is not yet conscious.

As Margaret's miasma stirs within David, it approaches his sphere of perception and he is faced with a choice: suppress the grief, experience the grief and then release it, help somebody who has already experienced the grief to overcome their pain and then follow their example or heal it energetically.

By suppressing the grief David will express it in other ways, such as the situations he encounters or via physical dis-ease. By physically experiencing the grief, David may take many months or even years healing himself from the trauma of his experience, however by choosing the route of the therapist or PsyQ consultant, David is offered a chance to heal himself before he is even aware of his pain.

One day, David meets a fragmented intelligence he names Caroline. He interprets Caroline through his own sphere as a person who lost a child and spent many years grief-stricken before eventually dying of consumption. Caroline's deep-rooted pain resonates with David and he fears her because she represents his own grief, so he ignores her existence. His logical mind tells him this ghost is a figment of his imagination.

The meeting with Caroline, however, has brought his own hidden grief further to the surface of his sphere and in time, he begins to attract incidences that leave him feeling the grief. It is this pain that leads the unsuspecting David to PsyQ development, so that he can develop his PsyQ senses.

In doing so he meets Caroline, but this time he is very much aware of her and decides to help her to overcome her pain. David learns how she transcends the residual grief from her life and uses that same style to heal his own subtle residuals of Margaret's grief.

In this fictional example, we see that our lives our filled with choices. By actively taking responsibility for our subliminal energetic connections we can actually develop ourselves and help others at the same time.

The benefits of rescue work are not just confined to our painful ties, because by working with lost souls we can bring our powerful connections to the surface and learn how to live our lives to the absolute fullness of our ability.

Of course, the above is not intended as a definitive account of all the complexities and variations of our subtle connections and spirit encounters, but more as a way of understanding rescue work as an integrated approach to our individual development rather than a random and separate methodology.

If we look at the traditional view of lost soul work, we understand that what we are doing is helping spirits that exist in limbo, or are somehow trapped by their circumstances, to the light of everlasting peace. It is a useful exercise to gain an insight into how this view of rescue work corresponds with the ideas or ethos of this Home Experience journey.

The initial similarities between an entity merging with an omnipresent light and the projection of a particular form of energy towards the spirit we are focusing upon, offer us a place to start. The state of limbo is often viewed as a place that is between realms, where a spirit is unable to find peace and is therefore condemned to walk the earth, undetected by many and ignored by most.

The role of the rescuer in traditional terms was to act as a conduit between the state of limbo and the realm of heaven, bliss or *the source of all things*. By enabling the spirit to *cross over*, the psychic assisted them in finding their everlasting peace and tranquillity.

In modern terms, we know that energy exists outside of space and time and so is, to all intents and purposes, infinite. If we understand the conscious experience to be in time and space, we see any consciousness that was unable to move from one energetic state to another would be in limbo or somehow trapped in the time-confined experience of timelessness.

However, when we project a variant energy pattern, we create a practice called entrainment—this we shall discuss in greater detail later upon our journey. The entrainment process alters the lost facet or *entity*, so that it can consciously experience other layers of energy.

To think that the consciousness then remains at that pattern in their perception of time would be misguided because an unchanging connection to any form of energy is limbo, even if that energy feels good!

Evolution and ascension are the routes to bliss and it is the *movement* that creates the bliss state, not the staying still. So our projection forms a catalyst for the lost facet to evolve, to become something other than that which they were. This does mean that when we are working to *rescue* a lost facet, we do not remove them or put them somewhere or even change their situation. We set in motion a healing process that instigates the growth and transcendence of the spirit.

As a lost facet entrains to layers of energy beyond our perception they fade from our awareness, although they are still there, simply perceiving the world from a different perspective. This means that in our time experience they can still be sensed on future occasions except that, in these instances, they are no longer in their limbo state.

The element of this discussion that really confuses people is when we come to the issue of an experience through time, because although you have healed an entity in your time experience, it is quite possible for another person to experience the facet you have previously cleared at a future time and in the state they were in before you helped them transcend.

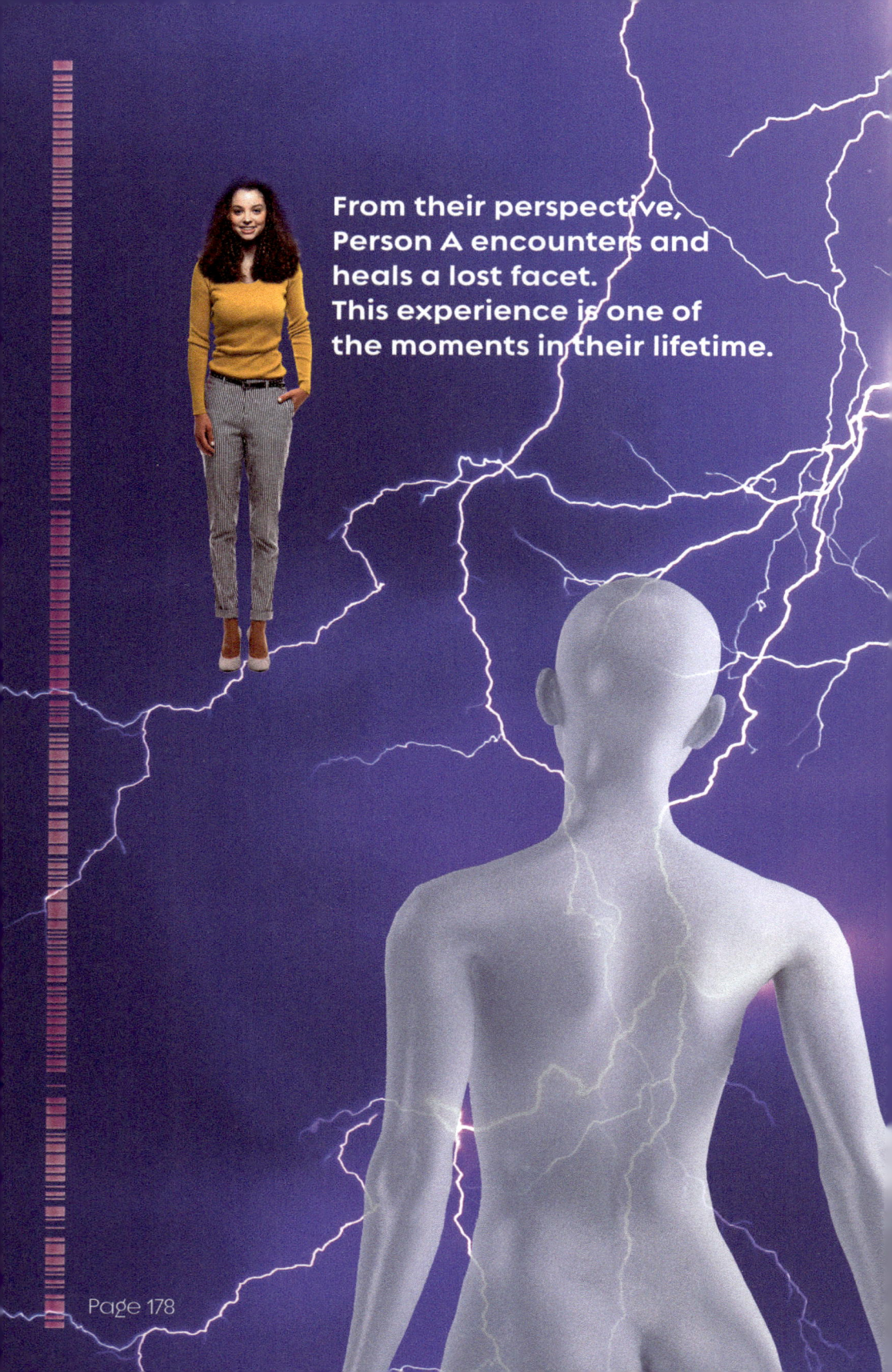

From their perspective,
Person A encounters and
heals a lost facet.
This experience is one of
the moments in their lifetime.

At a later date, Person B encounters the same lost facet from their perspective. Person A has already encountered and healed this facet, so does not experience the facet in the same way as Person B.

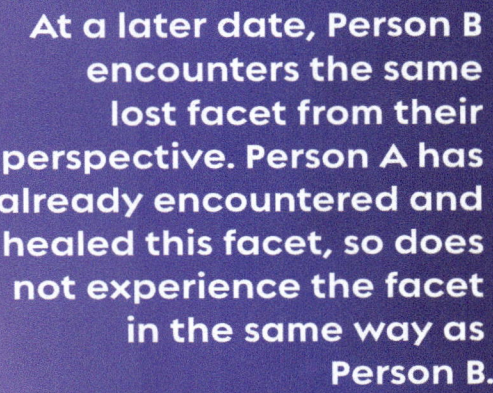

This does not mean that they have returned to their limbo—it means that the other person has connected into the original energetic state of the entity and is living the same *experience* as you but in a different *time* to you.

This often translates to a situation when you conduct events on several occasions in the same location but with different people, you may find them sensing an entity that was rescued the week before.

This is not a bad thing; it simply means that they have the same energy dynamics as the spirit in its limbo state. Repeating the process will not only help the person in the group, it will also heal the entity from a different perspective—and as we know, in energy work perspective is everything!

The communication and terminology associated with the traditional and modern perspectives of rescue work are very different. Very often this becomes an area of heated debate as to whether a certain term is the correct jargon or if an entity can actually understand modern terminology.

The question of whether a seventeenth-century farmer is able to comprehend the modern phrases and terminology we use, is both subject to debate and a moot point. The question is; why should a seventeenth-century farmer hear what you are saying at all? He has no ears and is not interacting verbally with anybody!

The lost are formed from vibrations and interaction with these vibrations change our own vibrational experience. These changes convey messages and intents. Any verbal communication we experience is focused upon our benefit and that of the people you are working with.

Of course, linguistically, jargon and terminology is important when referring to a particular subject. For instance, technical jargon in the IT industry is vital to the communication between people, as is Christian theology in the priesthood.

Yet, when we are debating energy, which has no defined boundaries and is something we cannot comprehend in anything more than three dimensions, we recognise that limiting terms are not helpful.

Using the rescue kit detailed in Appendix A, you can adapt your treatment methods from living people to the lost facets of energy you encounter. This method is actually much easier to perform, because you are working completely energetically, rather than practising with people in the physical world.

To understand the process and techniques of rescue world, explore the realms and experience the demonstrations available within.

Chapter Summary

Do You Know?

Understand the following methods and their uses:

- The Rescue Kit Essences
- The Rescue Kit Techniques
- The Tongue/Perineum Link
- The Energy Cultivation Technique

How combining essences and techniques works and how combinations can be applied to actual situations and circumstances.

Grasp the comparisons between the modern and traditional views of rescue work, especially the idea that working with the lost is connected to personal healing and development.

Chapter Homework
& Exercises

ONE: ESSENCES

Practise triggering the essences and finding ways of describing the sensations of each and the differences between essences. Attempt to combine essences and see how the amalgamation of two or more essences alters the sensations—are they merely a mix of two or more essences or are there differences in the way that a combination behaves?

TWO: TECHNIQUES

Practise working with the various techniques, noting differences between the different tools and your reactions to a single person, situation, etc. When you project a variety of techniques at the solitary focus—does it alter the way you perceive the person, situation, etc.?

THREE: COMBINATIONS

Work with the blending of essences and techniques—make notes on your findings and provide your tutor with these notes, either via the forum or via a hard copy.

FOUR: CONTINUATIONS FROM PREVIOUS CHAPTERS

Continue to work with your linguistic approach, monitoring the words that you use in connection with yourself and your PsyQ practices. Work with the RGB exercise, alpha/theta states, as well as continuing to conduct and add to your AT Routine. Finally, continue your breathing exercises, either separately or as part of other practices.

APPENDIX A

The Energetic Rescue Kit—
Essences and Shapes

We now look at a range of techniques, as well as different vibrations of energy, often referred to as *essences*. These essences were originally used in the treatment of people as part of the complementary therapy, *Lemuria*.

These particular essences exhibited such excellent results in treatments that they were tried and tested beyond the human experience, with lost entities and continued to yield great success. Here we can use these upon ourselves in self-treatment, with people in professional treatments and in rescue work with the lost.

Having a collection of essences and techniques that can be combined and adapted to suit, we discover a very efficient way of working with the needs of any situation we encounter. Thus follows your energetic treatment and rescue kit that can be viewed a little like a box of chocolates; you will have your favourites and those you do not like. You need not use everything included here, just what you enjoy using and, in time, you will adapt your repertoire and add to it.

Essences

Sandalwood

Comforting, Soothing, Releasing, General Use Rescue

This essence was harvested from the essential oil of sandalwood and has a wide sphere of action. Generally comforting, it soothes the mind, body and soul, enabling us to release any tensions or subconscious attachments that are currently holding us back.

In rescue work, the results are very much the same, yet here the essence has additional features that denote greater success in all-round repatterning of those lost for some reason.

Excellent at releasing many forms of painful emotion, sandalwood also helps to clear the dependencies the lost may have to those emotions as residues from their experiences. So, if an entity is trapped by the connections to its feelings in body or still maintains the habitual responses it has developed, sandalwood will work to release it from these ties.

Thus, sandalwood can be seen as a general-action essence that we often refer to initially when helping to repattern vibrations. It is particularly valuable when working with discordant vibrations.

Sandalwood will not work on these more powerful beings and the deeper-acting essences of greater potency are not as pleasant for the lost. In these circumstances, sandalwood will clear those initial lost facets in readiness for the application of plutonium or similar.

Salt

Purifying, Cleansing, Suppression, Unable to Express Emotions

Used in physical terms to cleanse and heal, salt also provides us with a superb purifier in energetic spheres, acting particularly well in the realms of suppressed feelings and thoughts. Now, while sandalwood is a soothing essence, salt is harsher in the way it works, practically forcing the emotions that need attention to the surface—when used with facets of sentient experience this can often be felt as explosive emotion.

Throughout history there has been a huge amount of suppression, not only in the dominion of emotions, but also with religious denomination, spirituality, love, sexual orientation, health, disease and many other areas that were once deemed to be unacceptable and had to be controlled in some way.

The need to hide one's true nature at all cost has created many facets of energy that hide or feel inadequate. They lurk in the darkness, in the shadows, wanting so much to be accepted but remain unable to find that acceptance.

Salt will bring these facets to the surface, so that sandalwood or rose can then be applied in the usual way. Salt can also be used to repattern locations or areas of disruptive facets and energy that causes contractive reactions, including that of the destructive dynamics that form between people.

ROSE

SOFTENS THE PAIN OF UNREQUITED LOVE, LOVE LOST OR GRIEF

Love is one of the major reasons that facets of energy become lost—if you have ever had a dream where you are unable to reach those you love and care for, you will have glimpsed for a brief moment the perspective of the entities that are so bound to a location that they cannot reconnect to those they want to be with.

It is good to remind ourselves that when a facet is in one particular state of energy, that state is eternal and it is only by altering that state that change occurs. When a person is so lost in unrequited love or grief that they cannot see beyond it, this facet will remain as a legacy in a specific physical place or places until a change is made.

Rose is one of the gentlest essences that subtly carry those who are fragile or emotionally delicate to the surface in order for you to help them. Alleviating the pain they feel will cause them to seek out the source of this relief and create a strengthening of the connection between them and you. Once this has occurred you can continue to work with rose or change to sandalwood in order to complete the repatterning process.

JET (JET MINERAL)

GRIEF, SORROW, TRAUMA OF DEATH, LOSS, VICTORIAN FACETS

Whenever we experience the loss of somebody or something treasured, we go through a period of grieving in order to heal. Sometimes that process goes beyond healing and the emotion of grief itself becomes something to block out the loss.

When grief transcends love and becomes a state in its own right, favouring sorrow and pain as opposed to the object of loss, we turn to jet.

This essence was harvested from a piece of the mineral, highly prized by the Victorians and as such it tends to work extremely well with vibrations sculpted from that era.

it is also a remarkable essence when used in relation to facets that are so connected to a trauma that they cannot see past it. whenever we come into contact with those who are unaware of their trauma or are in some other way traumatised by the process, we can apply jet as a way of healing and releasing without the need for other essences.

Vacuum

Asphyxiation, Drowning or Other Breathing Difficulty

Vacuum has proved to be a highly effective essence in rescue work, if a very specialised one. Working solely on the chest area in people, this translates to any facet who has placed the focus on lack of air. Using this extraordinary essence eases strangulation, hanging, drowning, suffocation or chest-related-illnesses, including heart attacks.

Often applied in conjunction with another essence, such as rose/ jet, yellow, sandalwood or oak/rowan, vacuum presents relief from the trauma of asphyxiation so that underlying connections can be broken. Hence, vacuum is frequently used alongside detailed communication with the facet or entity you are working with, in order to discover the most valuable prescription.

Yellow (Yellow Light)

Dark, Lonely, Depressing, Stagnant, Still, Lethargic

The essence of yellow is very similar to sunlight, yet without the cooler blues, violets and the more aggressive reds and oranges. It therefore provides the vibrancy and invigoration of the sun without any of the other effects.

Hence, yellow is a wonderful essence whenever we are working is places of darkness and stagnation. Those locations where people do not tend to go because they usually end up feeling drained or otherwise intimidated are ideal candidates for yellow.

Yellow is also an excellent essence for environments that cause the sensation of being drained or create depression. The energising qualities of yellow help to revitalise and boost the vibrancy of a location.

Excellent for the situations that are traditionally known as incidences of *vampirism*, this essence also helps assist assertion and is very beneficial when used to boost the vigour of the rescuer or consultant when feeling tired.

SILVER

CONFUSED OR HECTIC VIBRATIONS, RELIGIOUS DOGMA, PERSPECTIVES FROM 1550-1650

Settings that are comprised of many confused entities, hectic vibrations and a general energetic cacophony call for silver—the essence of harmony and order. For silver does not calm and pacify facets of energy, it aligns vibrations, so that the level of energy (amplitude) remains the same, whilst the chaos is tamed.

Hence, silver helps us sense passed the noise, to reach the quieter entities that may have become lost in the commotion.

Steeped in tradition, and an integral part of folklore, silver is also of great use when working with entities that are dogmatic or victims of religious dogma. For example, facets associated with witchcraft trials or execution, those persecuted for their religious beliefs or heresy. Consequently, silver has particular relevance to facets sculpted by the temporal period between 1550-1650.

Oak

Doorways and Portals, Weakness, Drained, Lack of Strength, Back Pain

Oak is the opener of doors and assists in the strengthening of connections. A highly supportive essence, it offers vitality to the weak and the beings that have lost their connection to a plentiful experience of energy.

Oak creates a secure and safe haven for the vulnerable and the frightened, working particularly well with children who have lost their parents, their way and their childhood. The essence is also very beneficial for the experience of debilitating illness, suffering much pain and physical weakness.

Oak is also an excellent essence to use in combination. For example; used with rowan to support the assertive qualities or with rose to create a balance of strength and softness. Yellow will create vibrancy in the strength of oak, while plutonium will add an enveloping disconnection to the combination, enabling it to cut through trauma or contractive reaction vibrations.

When used on the rescuer or consultant, oak will also help with back pain and other physical symptoms created from the interaction of vibrations.

Iron

Boundaries, Disconnection, Clearing of Residuals and Unwanted Vibrations

The essence of iron creates boundaries and thus enables disconnection from the surrounding energetic vibrations. Of course, these boundaries are merely an illusion created from the forceful, dense characteristics of iron. It has been used for centuries as an *etheric disruptor* (disrupting of energetic vibrations).

This essence is an excellent repatterning agent that will frequently wipe away unwanted vibrations, clearing residuals and eliminating unwanted *patterned energy*. (This is energy that is joined to a building, etc., as opposed to vibrations that are being emitted from a constant source. Therefore iron will work on the energy of past trauma, but will only achieve a temporary effect when used on the constant vibrations of an air-conditioning unit or similar.)

ROWAN

ASSERTION, STRENGTH, "DEMONS/ELEMENTALS" AND "EVIL"

The rowan tree was traditionally seen as a guardian against evil that would stop any person or spirit that meant ill towards another from carrying out that unpleasant intent. The essence of rowan continues this theme of assertion by providing strength and security for the user.

We are beginning to understand in modern Western society that evil is merely a term applied to those of different perspective, particularly when actions based upon that difference causes harm to people that share our perspective. In line with this, rowan deals with differences of perspective, particularly when those differences are in some way harmful to us.

Facets that reflect back our deepest fears and darkest traumas (traditionally known as demons or elementals) can indeed cause harm, although this is always psychologically based rather than actual, physical harm.

For example, there are entities that can create temporary repatterning of our perineural system to create the sensation of a heart attack; this can only ever be done if the recipient knows the energy of a heart attack already (via ancestry, etc.). The person is not physically suffering a heart attack, but the common reaction to the sensation is panic-based and thus harmful.

Rowan will assert against these psychological attacks and resulting energetic manipulation. Now, while it is beneficial for us to work with our hidden traumas and vulnerabilities, when the experience becomes too sensually overwhelming, it is not helpful. It is in these instances that rowan comes into its own.

PLUTONIUM

DARKNESS, ATTACK, PANIC, FEAR, DREAD, REPATTERNING

Plutonium is an essential part of any energetic rescue kit—it is fast acting and very efficient at creating total disconnection from any entity or energy that we focus our projection upon. Instead of creating a repatterning effect, which is often anticipated, it simply creates two different energetic states that are unable to affect each other.

One of these states exists in your perception, the other in the facet's perception. This incompatibility simply causes the entity to disappear from your awareness and you from theirs.

This means that, if an entity acts in an intimidating manner or causes you fear, etc., instead of projecting a *protective* vibration the entity is expecting and possibly be ready to counteract, you just disappear from its perception.

This same result can be achieved with other facets of energy including those connected to emotions, subconscious facets, etc.

18HZ

EYE AND FRONTAL LOBE PRESSURE, VISUAL DISTURBANCES, BEING WATCHED

18Hz is a very significant frequency in rescue terms because it produces pressure on the eyes and frontal lobes of the brain thus generating visual distortion and a feeling of being watched. Whenever you encounter an entity that forms heightened visual activity and creates the sensation of watching, you may want to verify the 18Hz effect.

By producing the equal frequency, out-of-phase shift (the peak on one vibration matches the trough of the other), you negate the waveform from physicality and thus stop it from having any effect on you.

This is particularly useful if you are susceptible to headaches caused by 18Hz vibrations (pain behind the eyes or in a band around the temples and forehead).

TECHNIQUES
THE BEAM

The Beam is a basic projection technique that creates a single perspective band or thread of energy between you and your focus. You could look at this as being a simple connection between you; the connection consisting of whatever essence(s) you are working with at the time.

To create a beam, simply focus on your subject and project the chosen essence to that point, rather like the distance/direct projection techniques. A perineum/tongue link will also help strengthen the connection.

THE PULSE

The *Pulse* expands upon the beam technique to generate a more elaborate connection that not only extends in every physical direction, but also produces greater force in vibrations you are working with. By bunching the vibrations into areas of little amplitude and larger amplitude, you can offer greater potency to your projection method.

The pulse is conducted using the same technique as the beam, except here, you coordinate one-second projection and perineum/tongue links, with one-second non-projection, with perineum/tongue released.

THE SPIRAL

When we project our experiences as a *spiral*, it creates the effect of heightening the potency of the projection, increasing the amplitude of the vibrations that are projected from one point to another.

     To conduct the spiral, simply visualise the essence rotating around you in an ever-increasing circumference, until it reaches the point of focus.

     When this is achieved, simply continue to project the essence along the arc of the spiral.

THE ECHO

The *Echo* is a little more complex in its workings, because as you visualise the projection of vibrations in all directions, these travel back towards you. As this dual movement is done in phase shift, it increases the potency of the vibrations for the duration of the projection and within the sphere of the projection.

This creates an effect similar to that of the spiral, with greater power.

To produce the echo, visualise a sphere around you and project vibrations in all directions to the surface of the sphere. When you see the energy reach the sphere in your mind's eye, project it back towards you. Once it has made the return journey, repeat the routine again, increasing the power of the energy each time.

THE TRIANGLE

By projecting energy from one point to another, via the third point, we create a style of vibration that is best suited to problem-solving and resolving issues in a physical environment. The energy passes through both the *focus* of the problem and *resolution* of the problem, before returning to the original point as a solution.

By creating this dynamic within our energy projection, we lay a foundation on which the physical can be constructed and clear the path for the situation to be resolved.

The *Triangle* is relatively straightforward to work with; simply project vibrations to your focus (problem), then from there to the second focus (solution), then bring the projection back to you and receive the solution.

The Arena/The Sphere

We have worked with the concept of an *Arena* previously, both in the idea that the realms exist within an Arena and you have an individual Arena to use when you practise.

The Arena projection or sphere adaptation, can be used in conjunction with essences to encapsulate, isolate/neutralise and assert energy. By projecting vibrations in an Arena/Sphere style, you create focused vibrations that do not react with their own energy connections.

Hence you envelop the focus of our projection in a non-reactive experience that both isolates and offers intense projection within that isolation.

The technique for creating the Arena projection is as that used for forming your Arena environment, while the sphere is simply visualised and saturated with the essence of your choice.

THE HYPERCUBE

The *Hypercube* (tesseract) works on the premise that energy exists in many more dimensions that we can perceive; yet we can use vibrations of energy as a way of reaching and altering those dimensions.

We operate in three spatial dimensions and encounter circumstances and situations that are also viewed through that 3D perception. If we can change the energy patterns of the three dimensions, plus alter a fourth spatial dimension, we act on the elements that we cannot perceive or change using the usual routes.

A hypercube cannot be understood in three dimensions, but we can create a representation of it, by thinking about a cube, within a cube; both connected at the corners.

The inner-cube is surround by six additional cubes, one at each of its faces, (one above, one below, one to the left, one to the right, one in front, one behind). These six cubes exist within the outer-cube, the outermost faces of the six cubes, forming the outer-cube.

Therefore we see that the inner and outer faces of the six cubes, which are also integrally connected to each other at every face, create the hypercube; this forms the illusion of the inner- and outer-cubes.

To create the hypercube, form the first cube just as if you were creating your Arena, then form a second energy cube between your hands.

Link the corners of your first cube, to the corresponding corners of the second. Expand the second cube until you are sitting inside of it and at the same time, shrink the first cube to match the size of the second.

With the two cubes at the same size, begin to shrink one cube down to your hands and expand the other, then repeat the process of shrinking and enlarging the cubes to the same size and so on.

COMBINING ESSENCES AND SHAPES

When we combine a particular flavour of energy (essence) with a certain methodology (shape), we not only alter the type of vibration we project but also the way in which we project it. These combinations form a vast range of different possible outcomes for a huge array of situations, when working with the lost, in treatment and other circumstances.

The way of triggering a combination is very basic, yet it can be adapted to help you gain clarity in your visualisations. So, by repeating the name of the essence three times and projecting the resulting vibrations using the routines above, you have a combination.

However, you could enhance this by visualising a proxy for each essence (rose petals for rose, acorns for oak, etc.) and a symbolic representation for each shape (a cube for Arena, ripples in a pond for pulse and so on).

As you integrate your rescue work and treatment practice, you will become more and more proficient at working with your healing and rescue kit, to the point where you simply trigger the required essence and shape combination.

This is the ideal situation, as it removes the need for clunky visualisations and processes—the less you need to think about a process, the more energy you have to offer the process itself!

Appendix B

THE LINGUISTIC APPROACH

Whilst terminology is often seen as an important part of psychic development, linguistics is usually ignored. However, when we consider the words we use in PsyQ development can actually improve or hinder our receptivity to vibrational fields, it becomes a priority to ensure that our linguistic approach is improved.

Nearly all the words we use create reactions at a physiological level in the body. These reactions affect us in various ways and could be equated with ripples in a pool of water, spreading outwards and creating further ripples.

An example of this could be the word *dangerous*; if somebody tells you that a practice is dangerous, your subconscious and physiological reactions may cause you to be nervous about undertaking that practice and therefore affect the way you do it. If that same practice were described as *joyous*, you would inherently become more relaxed as you conducted the practice.

Some of the terminology used in traditional psychic development is quite detrimental to sensory practices and there are other terms which can knock your confidence and sensory abilities to virtually zero!

Closely related to linguistics is the imagery we use as part of the development process. If the visualisations we use are based upon positive polarity language, we will be more likely to get better results and feel safer. If the imagery is based upon contractive polarities, we may feel unable to sense things and can even feel afraid or vulnerable.

So it is important to work with positive polarity words (words that create positive reactions) at all times. What are positive polarity words? Well, there is such a huge range of positive (and contractive) polarity words that it would impossible to list them here. However we shall be looking at some examples during the course, with two examples listed here.

CONTRACTIVE POLARITY:

- Protection
- To protect oneself
- Visualising a shell or cloak

The above are all contractive polarity, because they encourage the idea that we need to protect ourselves from something. We only ever protect ourselves from things that are bigger and stronger than we are or that are unknown and intangible.

By using the word *protect*, you are automatically placing yourself in a weakened position. If you add to this a shell of light or cloak visualisation, you are creating imagery that can be penetrated easily or removed from you.

EXPANSIVE POLARITY:

- Assertion
- To assert oneself
- Visualise light or energy that radiates from within

When we assert ourselves, we are usually doing so with an equal—usually human—and thus, are creating the reactions that say, "I am in a strong position here." This will subconsciously make you stronger and more assertive.

When the visualisation comes from within and radiates outwards, it cannot be taken from us or penetrated.

CONTRACTIVE POLARITY:

- Negative energy
- Energy that is bad for you

Energy is energy is energy. This phrase is very important, because there is no such thing as negative energy. Negative energy literally means that something has a negative amount of energy—this in turn leads to the falsehood that something can exist without energy or even with a deficit of energy.

No form of ELF energy is bad for you or has negative results— it is your reaction to energy that causes the effects you may not find comfortable or enjoyable.

EXPANSIVE POLARITY:

- Contractive reaction energy
- Energy that causes a painful reaction

A vibration of energy that causes you to feel sick, emotional or frightened, may cause somebody else to smell roses or feel wonderfully happy. Hence your reaction to any given aspect of energy is what is important here.

Contractive reaction energy or energy that causes a painful reaction has a greater degree of accuracy and is rather empowering. Plus it instils the understanding that by changing your perspective you can change your reaction to the energy you connect to.

Appendix C

An Anatomy of the Brain States

Our brain functions are integral to a high PsyQ; at any given time, our perception of the world(s) around us is experienced by our brain and will differ greatly depending on whether brain activity is high or low.

Scientists have established a quantifiable set of *brainwave states* that can be recorded via an EEG and give us the frequency of brain activity. Traditional science works with four brain states, which are:

- Beta
- Alpha
- Theta
- Delta

There are four additional brainwave states, which are becoming increasingly recognised by researchers. These are entitled:

- Epsilon
- Gamma
- Hyper-Gamma
- Lambda

Each brainwave state can be described both numerically, in hertz, which tells us the frequency of the brain activity, and symptomatically, describing the experiences of the person displaying that brain state.

Beta (12-40Hz)

Alertness, Concentration, Cognition

In the beta state, neuron activity in the brain is abundant, with regular and rapid firing of the neurons. This translates to a highly focused and attentive state, which provides the ability to work with full attention and peak mental ability.

Adaptive and sharp, new ideas form quickly and easily, thus enabling high levels of problem-solving ability, rapid learning and excellent analytical skills. When added to the heightened hand-eye coordination, beta state can also help improve physical performance and the ability to play sports.

As we approach the high beta state of 40Hz we begin to see signs of cognition and heightened awareness and we begin to access the higher conscious brain functions.

ALPHA (7-12HZ)

Relaxation, Visualisation, Creativity

Alpha state is the place of complete and blissful relaxation, where we are fully conscious, yet able to pay close attention to our subconscious abilities. With increased awareness and creative energy, we feel liberated, free and yet at peace with ourselves and the world around us. Our fear vanishes and we experience immense feelings of vitality and wellbeing.

Whereas beta can assist problem-solving to logical or practical issues, alpha aids problem-solving in creative ways; when the ability to be unorthodox is necessary. It thus helps with creative visualisation and to attain deep levels of creativity that lie beyond our normal consciousness.

Essential to our holistic health, alpha state can help us de-stress and remain calm, whilst placing us in line with the Schumann Resonance, which is the frequency of the earth's electromagnetic field.

THETA (4-7HZ)

Meditation, Intuition, Memory

Our theta state is a magical *dreamlike* state of consciousness, where we travel to just before the point of sleep. Neurological activity in the brain slows to the point that enables us to experience dreamlike imagery, deep insight and access age-old memories.

Associated with meditation states, theta state expands our awareness beyond the body, beyond the self to the limits of consciousness, thus enabling abilities such as ESP and psychic awareness, photographic memory and super-learning, in which we can learn subliminally.

Used in repatterning behaviour, such as overcoming habitual responses or addictions, theta state is used in hypnosis to allow the brain to redesign itself in a psychological and cerebral sense. Theta creates sensations of weightlessness, flying, astral travel, waking dreams, karmic memories: it is the true state of the shaman.

DELTA (0.5-4HZ)

Detached Awareness, Healing, Sleep

These slow, undulating waves of brain activity are often recognised as the lowest form of brain activity and represent the state that we shift into when in deep sleep. The delta state triggers the human growth hormone and enables the body to heal itself, thus working with delta offers the benefits of deep, refreshing sleep.

Useful whenever we wish to access the very heart of our intuition and expanded awareness, delta state provides deep insight from the very foundations of consciousness mind—meaning those at a group or soul level.

Epsilon (0.01-0.5Hz)

Ecstasy, Out-of-Body Experience, Astral Travel

Using the EEG in traditional brainwave studies has meant that research was limited to above the 0.5Hz range, as EEG machines are normally configured to monitor from this point. Recent research, however, has looked at meditation and yogic awareness using EEG equipment, set up to monitor the range from just above zero to 0.5Hz.

Here we see a brain state that is so low, physiological functions, such as breathing and heart rate, slow to levels that can hardly be detected. Thus creating awareness that is completely detached from the self.

With this extremely relaxed state, we can literally fly out of our body, travelling vast distances and even through space itself. The epsilon state could be seen as what is often called The Void or The Abyss, as it is here, we meet the divine, whomever that may be.

Gamma (40-100Hz)
Hyper-Gamma (100-200Hz)
Lambda (200Hz+)

Holographic Consciousness, Telekinesis, Hyper-Intelligence

These rare, yet remarkable states of consciousness have been monitored in EEG results, despite creating a very different type of consciousness. Our brains cannot resonate at these high frequencies in the same way as they do in beta state, for example.

However, the areas of the brain that can reach very high levels of activity synchronise with each other, to create what is known as a holographic consciousness. This could be seen as a protrusion of extradimensional awareness in our 3D realm.

The higher brain states create many of the same effects as the epsilon state, producing extraordinary results and abilities. It is therefore theorised that there is a circular connection between the low and high frequencies of brain activity.

It is surmised that whilst areas of the brain cannot resonate at higher vibrations, if these areas can lower to epsilon, whilst other areas are at gamma/hyper gamma/lambda states, we can witness telekinetic events and vast intelligence/cerebral ability.

ADJUSTING BRAIN STATE

Improving PsyQ relies on a change of perception and this means adapting our brainwave state, for it is here that our perception of the world is translated into conscious thought. Whilst there are many physiological factors that influence our brain state, it is the end result of brainwave changes that we need to consider in relation to PsyQ development.

Whether we are using a technique that functions by creating physical changes in the body chemistry, thus changing the brain patterns, or whether we go directly to the brain and create change there, it is the brain function that is the important factor.

So, if you want to create a relaxed alpha state, you can use physically induced change, such as breathing techniques or you can go straight to the source by using sound waves to entrain your brain state to alpha rhythm.

The important thing to bear in mind here is that it is the techniques that work best with you which will prove to be most effective. So if you work with the techniques of this Home Experience and find some easier to use than others, you can simply apply those ones that work for you.

APPENDIX D

THE HEALING PRACTICE

THE CONSULTATION: AN INTRODUCTION

Treating people with any therapy can be a daunting process for any person at first, but with time and a little bit of experience you will find it a very rewarding and pleasurable experience. As you settle in to your role of PsyQ consultant you will become aware of the areas that require *tweaking* or the knowledge you need to gather.

With each new consultation, you will become more and more sure of yourself and your abilities and the way you work will become an intuitive and very professional practice. When starting out however, this is little consolation and sometimes the greatest hurdle for a person to climb over on the journey to professional therapist is the transition from student to practitioner.

One thing will make this transition much easier for you—practice! The more practice you can give yourself before setting up professionally, the smoother you will find the step from treating somebody in a *make-believe* situation to treating *for real*.

The only differences in these two scenarios are in your mind, for the processes applied in your practice sessions are the same as those in your professional consultations. It is more a question of building the confidence to believe that you can do it!

So how can we set about creating the confidence to ensure that you succeed in your goal of becoming an active and fulfilled practitioner? Well, skilful planning and organisation is always a very good foundation, so here we look at the preparation you need to start the consultation process.

A *client questionnaire* and *therapy plan* are vital methods of information gathering and focusing on the outcome of several treatments. These two pieces of paper are very important to you as a therapist as they are the basis of your consultation and start the foundation of your journey with an individual client. As well as the initial information you need, should the situation arise in which you need to contact your client or their GP, you will also have a starting point in the form of a brief medical history.

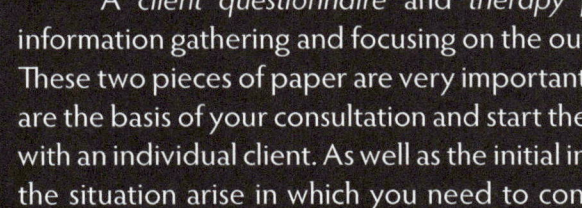

The therapy plan offers a regular and ongoing method of keeping the treatments on track so that you can create a clearer image of your clients' needs and individually tailor the consultations to those needs.

A new therapy plan can be started on each consultation session or you can produce a single plan for each issue your client wants to work with. You may even find that, for clients with more complex situations or for those who come to see you on a long-term basis, you may require a third sheet that catalogues and organises the therapy plans. This could be seen as an *overview* plan that ties up information across many therapy plans and assists you in keeping track of an individual's needs.

Another valuable item you may require is a checklist. While not essential, it is an excellent resource in the early stages of practice to ensure that you have given all the necessary pieces of information to a new client and have obtained everything you need from them. It is interesting to note how many new practitioners forget to collect payment for the consultation and think about it twenty minutes later!

On your checklist, you can include points such as: completed client questionnaire, completed therapy plan, checked contact details, clarified any information that is unclear from these forms, explained to client about your therapeutic practices, offered an overview to consultation structure, collected payment.

In time you will not need reminding as to the various items required, yet you may want to adapt your checklist into an *important points* sheet on which you can note any important points you need to clarify or follow up after a consultation. An example of this could be that you have doubts as to whether you should treat a client and need to write a letter to their GP.

It is important not to create paperwork for the sake of doing so and you may wish to combine sheets or aspects of the information contained across various forms. The more you limit your forms, the easier it will be in a live situation when you work through the different steps and need concise information quickly!

Over time you will adapt and change your forms so it is a good idea to start using these right from the outset. Becoming accustomed to the paperwork will enable you to handle and complete the forms in a fluid way, rather than shuffling bits of paper and searching through the questions. This will also help you to understand very quickly what (if any) changes need to be made in your paperwork.

Very soon you will find that you require files to keep your records in order. Organise a system that works for you from the very beginning and that can also be adapted in time. Do keep in mind that you must keep all documentation regarding your clients so, if you plan to use a computer to store data, you must keep the originals.

As a therapist, your time is valuable and whilst clock-watching is a definite no-no, you must ensure that your time is well spent, both in and between consultations. One of the more common issues faced by new therapists is when regular clients become more familiar and friendly and what should be an hour of feedback, discussion and treatment becomes three hours of chit-chat.

This is an issue that is very common and often reveals a deeper issue with the therapist who is unable to balance care and assertion. Unable to move the consultation onwards or lead the conversation to a close and yet unwilling to cut the client short; a novice can quickly become resentful and therefore is not at peak ability with that client.

We shall look at the dynamics of a consultation later, however, good timetabling and structure help you guide a consultation that satisfies both the needs of the client and the practitioner. As with checklists, the more you experience consultations the easier you will find it to gauge the time and structure of a consultation thus enabling a more natural flow to a session.

With practice you will hone your timetable and get into the routine of consultation structure and the work that is completed outside of a treatment session. Once you have created a routine, there will be little need for written timetables but, initially, it is good to have an idea of the necessary steps in consultation/client care/administration, so here are some suggestions.

We see that in the first case (*Timetable 1*), we have a leisurely plan that enables an hour consultation and treatment, with twenty minutes set aside for pre- and aftercare. In this scenario you can also have a twenty-minute break between clients to reflect, relax or do whatever you want to do.

In *Timetable 2*, we see a much shorter period of consultation/treatment time (forty-five minutes). This means that if you wanted to, you could see one client every hour. This is a more intensive timetable that some practitioners prefer to work to. Remember of course that, when working to this regime, you should allow time for breaks and lunch also!

You will probably find that your best timetable is somewhere between these two examples or possibly a mixture of the two. What is important is that these are not set in stone, they are merely a guide so that you can better steer the consultation/treatment process and work with greater integrity in the time given. By having an idea of how long you will require in a session, you can estimate when the time is approaching to move the conversation along or begin treating.

You should also be aware that even if you do not have many clients in a day, you should still have a rough timetable in your mind. There may come a time when you do have many clients and it is much easier to set the guidelines from the beginning rather than cutting down a three-hour consultation to an hour when things get busy.

In addition to the above, there are many other factors to consider when preparing to consult clients. These fall under the category of *setting up your practice* and will be dealt with later as we work through the setting up of your practice and the behind the scenes work involved initially and on a daily basis.

Before we continue with our investigation of the consultation process, here are some other points to consider:

- Where will you practise—home/treatment centre/office?
- Will you work specific hours—9am-5pm or evenings only, etc?
- Will you provide an emergency service for out of hours calls? This is a big commitment that requires a lot of thought.

- Is your practice to be separate from home life? For instance, will you block off set times for work (e.g., five days a week) or fit your practice around your other commitments?

- What do you propose to charge for treatments? And what costs do you incur?

- Are there other areas of expertise that you can bring to your treatment sessions or that you wish to learn to enhance your practice?

- Do you have any other training needs?

- Are you looking to provide a general practice or to specialise in the needs of specific clients? Some practitioners choose only to treat women/men/non-binary genders or focus on a particular type of situation such as emotional issues.

Timetable 1 – *1-hour consultation/treatment and 20 minutes pre/aftercare*

-10 minutes to –5 minutes:	Read through client's notes.
-5 minutes to 0 minutes:	Prepare room and self.
0 minutes to 2 minutes:	Ask client to enter/collect client, etc.
2 minutes to 15 minutes:	Obtain a verbal summary of how the client has been since the previous session and discuss. Then decipher what the intent of this treatment will be.
15 minutes to 55 minutes:	Treatment
55 minutes to 60 minutes:	Offer and obtain feedback on the treatment, bring consultation to close and show client out.
60 minutes to 70 minutes:	Make notes on aftercare and any other actions to take.

Timetable 2 – *45 mins treatment and 15 mins pre/aftercare*

-10 minutes to –5 minutes:	Read through client's notes.
-5 minutes to 0 minutes:	Prepare room and self.
0 minutes to 2 minutes:	Ask client to enter/collect client, etc.
2 minutes to 10 minutes:	Obtain a verbal summary of how the client has been since the previous session and discuss. Then decipher what the intent of this treatment will be.
10 minutes to 40 minutes:	Treatment.
40 minutes to 45 minutes:	Offer and obtain feedback from treatment, bring consultation to close and show client out.
45 minutes to 50 minutes:	Make initial notes of aftercare and any other actions to take.

THE INTRODUCTORY CONSULTATION

Let us now turn to the anatomy of an introductory consultation and treatment, gaining an understanding of how we can base future, ongoing sessions on this initial framework. The first time we meet and work with a client, the consultation tends to take up a longer period of time as it is important to explain a little about ourselves, the way we work and the philosophies of PsyQ treatments and the way these work to produce beneficial results.

We also take some time to explain the rough framework of a typical treatment (what will happen). There may be other elements of your practice that you wish to talk through with your client. For example, you may want to explain to your client where facilities are in the building or your policy regarding out of hours calls.

In addition to this, the first consultation (and perhaps some subsequent ones) will require some extra clarification and explanation pertaining to any detoxification the client may experience after treatment, as this will no doubt all be very new to your client. Apart from these aspects of the first consultation, the routine is very much the same from session to session and the steps will become familiar even if the dynamics of each occasion differ.

One of the most important things to remember throughout the first consultation is to be yourself in a professional capacity. Try not to be somebody you are not or act in a way that is alien to you—the reason your client has come to you is because you are the perfect therapist for them at this time. This is not down to the therapy you practise, per se, but due to you and who you are as a person. Neither you, nor your client may actually realise it at first, but in time you will understand exactly why you were brought together in this way.

Always remember to smile and be in a positive frame of mind but, apart from that, let your natural abilities and personality shine through. If you are generally a happy and humorous person, allow your clients to see this, if you tend towards a compassionate and more serious side, then bring this to the forefront. Find your strengths and let them come to the surface rather than create the stereotype of who you think a therapist *should* be.

Something that should be mentioned here is that we all have *off* days, but even when you feel grumpy, sad, stressed or in a very bad mood, do not let this overcome your positive skills and facets. It does not mean you have to gloss over your feelings, but ensure that your professionalism is always there to bring your positive side out and maintain it for the whole session. If you feel that you really cannot work with a client without letting the contractive stuff through, then you should consider cancelling the appointment—although, if at all possible, this should be avoided.

In the first meeting, your client is probably unaware of what is to come and what form their treatment is to take, so be aware of this and be prepared to answer any questions. It is often a good idea to ask if your client has questions at regular intervals, just to be sure they are not confused by anything you explain to them.

Clear, concise and interesting details about you and your therapy are very important, so we shall look at what needs to be explained and work through some exercises to do this.

- Introduce yourself and talk about your background
- Explain briefly about PsyQ healing and its philosophies
- Describe how you work and the framework of treatments
- Any questions?

Another interesting point to make at this juncture is that different people require differences in explanation as to why PsyQ or energy healing is so effective and how it works. Some clients may want to understand the physiological processes behind treatments, while others would find this form of description positively off-putting!

It is therefore good practice to understand your therapy from many different perspectives such as scientific, psychological, esoteric, metaphysical, simplistic, creative and so on. You will quickly come to recognise that, by monitoring how your individual clients speak and express themselves, you will identify the best way of explaining treatments as and when required.

So, for example, some people may want to understand the processes from the perineural system philosophy while others would prefer to work with the concepts of energy. Some people will absolutely refuse to believe that emotions could be created from chemicals, yet will understand perfectly when you describe the *emotional energy*—even if the former is widely accepted in the scientific community and the latter would cause the same scientists to laugh hysterically.

Some clients will ask more and more complex questions as they attempt to completely conceptualise the processes behind the treatments and some will need no more than a cursory explanation before treatment takes place! Hence, being able to quickly bring to mind various approaches towards the explanation of PsyQ/energy therapies is a valuable skill in consultations.

Once you have completed these areas of the initial consultation, you may want to discuss the client questionnaire. Take a brief moment to check that you can read all the details, you have a way of contacting your client quickly (phone number) and that their GP's details are listed.

Points to checklist here could be that you have:

- Run through the details and cleared up any issues here.
- Clarified and discussed medical history.
- Asked why the client has come to you.
- Asked what issues they particular want to deal with.

There may be times when you feel concerned or wary about working with a particular client for some reason. Common feedback from some therapists is in the area of mental illness, especially SDI (Suicidal Depressive Illness), schizophrenia and other forms of *personality disorder*. Now while in many cases there is no reason not to work with clients who have listed these diseases, it really comes down to your personal impressions and needs. If you ever feel at all uncomfortable or out of your depth, explain this to your client and say that you would require a GP/consultant's agreement before treatment can commence.

An excellent way of achieving this is to send your client a letter to take to their medical professional for them to sign and stamp. Your client can bring this back to you and you can place it in their file. The letter should explain what you practise and ask if the GP/doctor is agreeable to treatment. The medical professional should not be asked to provide details of their patient to you—only if they think it is safe for you to proceed.

Once you have completed discussion of the questionnaire, it is time to switch to the therapy plan and, having checked the contact information, begin to complete this. When your client has explained their issues and what they want to achieve from treatments, you can work with your client to create a precise (or at least focused) plan of what targets you are both looking to work towards: you in proposal of techniques and your client in the completion of those techniques.

Ongoing Consultations

When adapting your treatment timetable for returning clients you will be able to lessen the extent of explanation required as they get more accustomed to the methodology of treatment.

The timetable required for regular treatments will not require any of the initial questionnaire or introductory information. You will usually begin with a general catch-up and then get straight to treating your client.

With each consultation, be sure to make notes on the client's therapy plan that describe breakthroughs and areas of future focus. If you do have long-term clients, be sure to arrange regular reviews that monitor your client's progress and how they are feeling about their therapy. It is important to ensure that your client is happy about progress made and see if there are any changes they would like to make to their treatment.

Prescribing the Treatment

During the consultation process you can glean enough information to prescribe the best treatment for your client. Listening to your client in a non-judgemental way, yet deciding where the root of an issue may lie is a fine balancing act. But when it is perfected, your prescription skills will work wonders!

All dis-ease originates from spiritual/energetic layers that have filtered through to the psychological, emotional and physical layers. Thus we could treat all clients on spiritual levels. However, sometimes treatments that take this approach take time to filter through to the symptoms or may be hindered by the extent of a person's attitude or dis-ease.

So prioritising which level to work on is always a good idea. It is also important to to discover whether your client likes a hands-on (physical) treatment, a hands-off (just above the body) treatment or an auric (anywhere in the room) treatment. Decide whether you are going to use yellow light or rose? What techniques will you use?

At all times in the consultation, match what your client is really telling you with the techniques and facets of energy that are best suited to their needs. By the time you come to the treatment, you should have a very good idea of what you will be doing. Do also bear in mind that your intuition and PsyQ abilities are absolutely invaluable at this point!

The Fundamentals of Your Professional PsyQ Business and Practice

Creating and running your own business is any field is a complicated, vast and in many cases, bewildering process. Along the way you will encounter conflicting information, advice that is not the right advice for you and a need to keep going no matter what!

Business comes naturally to many people, for others, it can feel like an absolute grind, which is counter-intuitive and seemingly unnecessary. Especially in the field of the holistic arts, the business arena can appear as if it goes against everything stand for.

However, this is because the world of business currently rewards those who think a certain way, while others who are perhaps more altruistic in their approach are pushed aside. This, thankfully, is changing in very powerful ways.

Some of the world's biggest and most successful businesses are edging towards a new way of doing business—a deeply benevolent and compassionate form of business that holds lessons for us all.

When it comes to your business, chances are the corporate world will seem a million miles away, as you strive to creating something that is uniquely yours. And whilst you may choose to apply the ethos of many big business to your little business, being a small business owner is a learning curve that can push buttons which are directly linked to the core of your life.

Money, home, family and your personal reputation are all on line as you step forward, inch by inch, day by day. As bills flood in, time runs out and you happen upon those who seem to delight in putting you down, it is vital to maintain your resolve and, no matter the blips upon the way, keep adapting and marching onwards.

In the beginning you have two resources… time and money. Chances are that money is the lesser of the two, so invest your time well. Focus on the activities that create more than an hour's worth of value for an hour of your time. Focus on building your financial reserves, rather than spending them and ensure your time is paid for a quickly as you can.

In short, do not spend money on expensive business cards and leaflets. Their sole purpose is to give contact information and, in this endeavour, cheaply created cards will suffice. Rather, invest time in being of service to people and building a name for yourself, through word of mouth, in online communities or even a YouTube channel, Instagram or Pinterest board!

Truly valuing yourself is important in business, because you need the confidence to sell yourself and your abilities. From your training, your expertise, your experience and your life-gained perspective, you are not charging for one hour of time; you are charging people for everything you are and only you can be.

When you appreciate the real value of who you are and how precious every moment of your life is, you will understand how valuable you are. In time, the balance will shift from more time than money, to more money and very little available time to spare. When this occurs, you will need to learn how best to multiply your time and leverage the skills of others to grow your business.

There are libraries of books that offer advice of building a business in every field, including those which leverage your PsyQ; a good starting point is *The Key to Business and Personal Success*. This book is focused on holistic arts and using the very same tools to profile yourself and appreciate how best you will run a business without sacrificing your own, personal morals.

When it comes to the running of your business in the PsyQ arts, it is important to be professional, to work towards a greater purpose and to ensure you know you are fully-protected legally. This is absolutely vital when working with treatments, consultations and other PsyQ arts.

Each territory around the world has different laws and regulations. It is essential you are conversant with these in the territory or territories you are practising in. For example, knowing that you are properly insured, both as a practitioner and as a business, is a must!

Some national or local governments insist on certain qualifications (such as Anatomy and Physiology), to practise in a healing capacity. You may find that your area classes some PsyQ practices to be religious in nature, which may need you to be an ordained minister!

Whatever the particulars, it is your responsibility to know what the law is in your area of professional operation. The accountability for any wrongdoing or complaint stops with you, so ensure that you are best protected as a professional.

There are three big essentials when it comes to the law that are so important, we can class them as universally appropriate. When running a business as a professional practitioner in any PsyQ practice, never:

- Offer your client a diagnosis
- Claim to cure a terminal illness
- Break the code of ethics or the law in your territory

Only medical doctors and qualified general practitioners of medicine can diagnose dis-ease. If you do so, even when you are absolutely sure, or simply in passing, you are breaking the law and the ethics of accredited PsyQ consultancy.

Any claim to cure cancer is illegal in most places. Therefore, it is not only inappropriate, it can lead to imprisonment in some areas. To be absolutely sure of your professionalism and the legal position of your practice, avoid claiming to cure any terminal disease. Focus instead on the holistic benefits and overall wellbeing your practice can offer.

Finally, but not exclusively, each territory may have a code of ethics that is fairly standard from place to place, country to country. This will cover areas such as client confidentiality, client relationships, equality of care and discrimination, data protection and so on. You may also need membership of a professional body or ongoing qualification updates or continual professional development.

In many cases codes of ethics are voluntary, however you are strongly advised to know and adhere to any codes that apply to your profession in your territory.

The key to running a successful, professional and legal practice is to be informed and proactive in your approach. Take accountability and a zealous approach to evolving personally and professional. Saturate yourself in wisdom, knowledge and information that enables you to grow and be better skilled in your profession.

Keep informed of forthcoming changes to the law or regulations that affect the PsyQ arts and also, set yourself the goal of being the best business owner you can be, in your own way and with a passionate approach to success.

When you treat your business as a living entity that requires protection, nourishment, nurture and empowerment, you shift from running a business as a necessary evil to growing a business as a legacy.

Martyn Pentecost

Author and therapy originator, Martyn Pentecost, began developing One Therapy in 1998 with the creation of Celtic Reiki. Since then he has been continuously resculpting and expanding these modalities.

Along with various other forms of holistic therapy, such as the elements of One Therapy (Karmic Regression Therapy, vReiki, Celtic Reiki, Viridian Method and PsyQ) and Creative Writing Therapy (CWT), Martyn uses his Seership and storytelling to weave vast Home Experiences. These help people across the world to learn, grow and develop new professions through enchanting, immersive study programmes.

As a writer, Martyn has written more than twenty-five books, which encompass both fiction and non-fiction. Exploring therapy and personal development, as well as business books and Transmedia experiences, Martyn's ever-growing library of books seeks to present readers with very different, sometimes challenging perspectives on established ideas.

Seeking to transcend common misconceptions and problematic trends in society, Martyn uses his unconventional worldview to evolve change—helping others to establish new ways of living, through their own uniqueness and personal superpowers.

Above all, Martyn's mission is to be of service to those who seek a life of greater depth and understanding. His legacy is to provide those who are misunderstood, alone and different, with the tools to step into their own way of living with pride and strength... to disrupt the established norms that are actually not normal at all.

ONE THERAPY HOME EXPERIENCE

Five aspects of professional practitionership and consultancy, synthesised into *One Therapy*.

PsyQ is a vital element in a broader personal, therapy and professional development world. With *One Therapy*, Martyn Pentecost has originated each aspect of your adventure through the realms, built revolutionary resources and immersive training programmes.

One Therapy brings together *Celtic Reiki, Karmic Regression Therapy, vReiki, Viridian Method* and *PsyQ* into one, cohesive craft. With professional accreditation and community support, *One Therapy* is a holistic paradigm that shifts your world, your career and your life to a new dimension of experience.

You can discover much more about the various aspects of *One Therapy* at ***www.one-therapy.com***

OTHER ONE THERAPY BOOKS AND RESOURCES

Karmic Regression Therapy and Karmic Reiki:
Practitioner Manual
ISBN: 978-1-907282-19-5
Martyn Pentecost

vReiki One: Introduction to the Reiki Revolution
ISBN: 978-1-907282-61-4
Martyn Pentecost

The Viridian Method: Introduction to the Viridian Method
ISBN: 978-1-907282-25-6
Martyn Pentecost

The Celtic Reiki Home Experience
www.celtic-reiki.com

Lightning Source UK Ltd.
Milton Keynes UK
UKHW052019150721
387219UK00002B/4

Praise for *The Next Revolution in Branding*

Trust is vital to any brand, as Karin Sebelin articulates throughout *The Next Revolution in Branding: Becoming a Key Person of Trust*. Success is dependent on integrity, which must always be top of mind.
—**Dorie Clark**, strategy consultant, speaker, author of *Entrepreneurial You, Stand Out and Reinventing You*

To be a relevant personal, organisational or offering brand, you need credibility based on trust. Karin's book shows that trust that has been conceptualised and nurtured from multiple perspectives will be most likely to have the depth, strength and resilience to support a strong brand platform.
—**David Aaker**, vice chairman of Prophet, brand strategist, author of eighteen books on marketing, business strategy and branding

Trust is the most valuable currency in the 21st century. Yet the concept continues to be elusive. This book is packed with concrete principles and actionable advice. Karin Sebelin reveals how to boost your success by becoming a trustworthy individual, and a trusted and respected brand in business. Her advice will encourage you to think and motivate you to act. I strongly recommend this book.'
—**Frank Sonnenberg**, CEO of Sonnenberg & Partners, award-winning author of seven books including *Follow Your Conscience and Managing With a Conscience*

In this book, Karin Sebelin demonstrates that branding begins with trust. It's a valuable lesson for any marketer.
—**Nir Eyal**, consultant, speaker, bestselling author of *Hooked: How to Build Habit-Forming Products*